IDITAROD

Also by

PAM FLOWERS

Alone across the Arctic

Big-Enough, Anna

Douggie

Ordinary Dogs, Extraordinary Friendships

Ellie's Long Walk

Sojo

TOGO and Leonhard

IDITAROD
One Thousand Miles Across Alaska by Dog Team

PAM FLOWERS
Iditarod Finisher

A & A Johnston Publishing

Iditarod: One Thousand Miles Across Alaska by Dog Team

ISBN: 979-8-9852896-0-2

The typeface for this book was set in Times New Roman.

Design by Brent Spears - brentspears.com

Published by:

A & A Johnston Publishing

P. O. Box 188
Talkeetna, AK 99676
www.pamflowers.com

Distributed by:

Ingram
One Ingram Blvd
La Vergne, TN 37086

For Terrie Hanke
Iditarod Teacher on the Trail 2006
and all the thousands of teachers all over the world
who use the Iditarod Sled Dog Race to teach compassion and persistence

Acknowledgments

This book was made possible because of the combined efforts of many people
and eleven hard working, wonderful, dedicated sled dogs.

My deepest thank you to Earl and Natalie Norris who taught me
how to train and care for sled dogs and helped me grow from
a complete novice to a competent musher.

I want to offer my sincere thank you and appreciation to
Joanne Potts and Starre Szelag for providing useful information.
Becky and all the tech people at Sharp Photo in Eau Claire, WI for converting my
photos and slides into digital images, including those in terrible condition.
Terrie Hanke for her editing and insightful comments, photographs, and for
correcting errors in my story because no one knows the Iditarod like Terrie.
Judith Niemi for her invaluable editing and broadening of this book through
creative suggestions and for pointing out all those dangling participles.
Helen Hegener for proofing the text.
My gratitude to all the employees of Providence Hospital
who cheered for my dogs and me and for sponsoring a huge bake sale.
Thank you to the person who donated the walrus tusk cribbage board,
I wish I knew your name.
The Iditarod for allowing me to use their Iditarod Race Trail map.
Thank you Bob Chlupach for believing in me and my dogs and for your guidance.
Doyle Holmes, your lines and snaps literally kept my team together.
Thank you Kari (Skogen) Norris for being brave enough to ride the trailer sled.
Thank you all the volunteers and people who opened their homes
and all the commercial sponsors who support the race in so many ways.

Most of all thank you sled dogs Jocko, Tommy, Amy, Bobby, Moose, Sasha,
Sammy, Cletus, Hank, Ed, and Ernie for adding so much joy to my life.

Preface

IDITAROD - a name that conjures up thoughts of adventure, daring, and dog mushing. When I first moved to Alaska in the fall of 1981 to learn dog mushing, I had never heard of the Iditarod Sled Dog Race. After listening to the 1982 race on the radio, I became inspired and determined to be a part of the race the next year.

The Iditarod Trail is steeped in rich and dramatic history that began in the early part of the 20th century. For decades mail carriers, adventurers, and fortune seekers slogged along the Iditarod Trail from Seward to Nome, Alaska, mostly by foot or dog sled. In the mid-1920's airplanes gradually started taking over delivery of mail and transporting people around the state. By the 1940's the Iditarod Trail was abandoned. For a while some people still used sled dogs for hauling firewood and other small chores but in the 1960's dogs were replaced by snowmachines (that's Alaskan for snowmobile) and sled dogs almost vanished from Alaska.

Legendary Dorothy Page and Joe Redington, Sr. became determined to revive the use of sled dogs and to restore the Iditarod Trail. They began developing the idea of a thousand mile sled dog race from Anchorage to Nome, Alaska. Most people thought this was impossible, but through dogged persistence and hard work they pulled it off. The first Iditarod Sled Dog Race was held in 1973. Thirty four teams set out, and though only 22 finished, the race was a huge success and became an annual event. In 1978 Congress designated it The Iditarod National Historic Trail.

March, 2022 the Iditarod race celebrated its 50th anniversary! All the excitement had me thinking back to my 1983 journey to Nome and all those wonderful memories of sled dogs and mushers inspired me all over again. Like most mushers, I love telling a good story, so I decided to write this book to celebrate and share my own amazing trip on the Iditarod Trail. It's the story about how a tiny woman with little experience, almost no money, not much in the way of sponsors, along with sled dogs Jocko, Tommy, Amy, Moose, Cletus, Sasha, Sammy, Bobby, Ernie, Hank, Ed, trained and became a team that succeeded in finishing the Iditarod Sled Dog Race.

I hope this story inspires others to pursue their dreams whatever they may be, no matter size, gender, age, race, where you come from in society, or how many times someone tells you that you will never succeed. If you try and fail, don't complain, just get up and try again. Always, always keep your eye on your dream, because wherever you are looking, that's where you're going.

Contents

Somewhere on The Burn, March 10, 1983

Just after sunset a cold snap moves in and over the next four hours the temperature plummets to -30°F. Darkness makes the wind feel colder and I can feel the warmth slowly seeping out of my body. A sudden gust of wind hurls loose snow against my face, stinging my eyes. Then another gust and another and another until the entire right side of my face is plastered with icy snow. Freezing! I can feel my face freezing! I pay no attention to the trail as I frantically try to scrape the snow off with my mitten. Suddenly the sled lurches to a halt. I fumble with the switch on my headlamp. In the narrow beam of light, I squint into the blowing snow, trying to see why we have stopped.

Jocko, my number one lead dog, turns his head and looks back at me. He is a decisive leader and I know he would only stop if he doesn't know what to do. I pull my parka hood forward to shield my face and walk up beside him. His dilemma is immediately obvious. We are on top of a long, barren ridge and, right in front of Jocko, the trail splits in two. Both trails look evenly used.

The beam of my headlamp barely penetrates 50 feet into the snowy void. I can see no trail marker indicating which way to go, so I decide to leave the dogs and walk along the trail to see what I can find. Peering into the darkness, I head down the left trail first with the wind steadily pushing me from behind. After maybe a hundred yards I find no marker. When I turn around and head back toward the dogs, the wind blasts snow straight into my face. Every time I try to look ahead my eyes water and my eyelashes freeze together. Cold. I can feel my hands getting numb and my face is beginning to freeze again. I raise my arms to protect my face. Within seconds my arms feel numb half way up to my elbows. I'm scared at how cold I'm getting. The wind is so powerful, every step is a struggle and I feel as though I am smothering. I lean into the wind and try to quicken my pace.

When I finally get back to the dogs, they are all lying down with their backs to the wind and their noses tucked under their tails. Jocko raises his head and stares up at me with a look on his face that suggests he is expecting a decision. I'm so cold.

CHAPTER 1

How It All Began

Dogs. When I was growing up in the Upper Peninsula of Michigan, my family always had a pet dog. The one I remember most was a beautiful, sweet German Shepherd named Lady. She was a tiny puppy when my father brought her home sometime around my seventh birthday. I played with her for a while and then my mom and I took her down to the basement where we lined a box with a thick blanket to make a snug little bed for Lady. My mom fed her twice a day while I was assigned the job of making sure her water bowl was always full. Proud of my new responsibility, every morning I headed down to the basement with a pitcher of water and ceremoniously topped off Lady's bowl while reminding her that I would see her again when I got home from school. Because both my parents worked and my brother and I were in school all day, Lady spent much of her puppyhood alone in that basement. Looking back, I think Lady must have been a lonely puppy.

When she was old enough to live outside my dad built a big, wooden, dog house in our back yard and surrounded it with a fence to keep Lady from running off. She could see what was happening nearby and barked a lot, mostly I think because she was bored and wanted attention.

My neighborhood had blocks and blocks of streets lined with small, wooden houses surrounded by neatly manicured lawns. But in all those houses there were only three kids my age and within two years every one of them moved away. After that, I was a very lonely little girl, so gradually I began turning more and more to Lady for companionship. Every afternoon, as soon as I got home from school, I'd rush into the back yard where Lady sat patiently waiting. With her tail swishing gently back and forth, she would sit in rapt attention while I conducted our own private Show & Tell and described all the important events that had happened in school that day. If something happened that made me happy, I told her. If something made me sad or mad, I told her about that too. I kept no secrets and shared everything with Lady.

In 1955 something else happened that would influence me for much of my life. Once a week I began spending the evening sitting on the floor in front of our radio listening to a program about a guy named Sergeant Preston and his husky, King. The good Sergeant had a dog team and they traveled around Yukon Territory in Canada catching bad guys. The stories were so exciting that by the second episode I could see myself running a dog team along snowy trails, through freezing blizzards. I began making plans and explained to Lady that I was going to get a dog team and that she would be my lead dog. We would be brave and strong! Together we would right wrongs! We were going to be heroes!

Weeks flew by and after each episode of Sergeant Preston my plans grew bolder and more dramatic. Then one day after school as I raced into the back yard to tell Lady about my latest scheme on how we were going to become super-heroes, she wasn't waiting for me. I looked inside her dog house and there she was fast asleep on a bed of straw. She looked so peaceful. *Well, even super-heroes need to take a nap every now and then,* I thought, so I climbed in with her. She woke with a start! "It's okay, girl, it's just me." She arched her back, stretched her legs out, and went back to sleep. I snuggled down behind her, wrapped my arm around her chest, gave her a big hug, and whispered, "I'll tell you my plan later." Her tail thumped the floor once and together we drifted off to dreamland.

By now I had come to understand that, whenever I was with Lady, I wasn't lonely. She was someone I could count on, someone I could trust to always be there, and Lady was never too busy to pay attention to me. She was my friend, my best friend. Because of Lady I fell in love with dogs.

I think Lady would have loved being a sled dog. But of course as I grew older and life got in the way, the dream of chasing bad guys with a dog team gradually faded away. I finished high school, moved to Texas, graduated college, and spent the next several years working as a respiratory therapist. Then in 1980 I set out on a car-camping trip around the United States that ultimately brought me to a temporary house sitting stint and a part time job as a respiratory therapist at a hospital in Northern Virginia.

Is there such a thing as Fate? Is your entire life planned out for you by some all-powerful force? I don't know the answers but I do know that my life took a sudden and unexpected turn in the summer of 1981. While thumbing through a magazine I'd bought at a bookstore, I came across an article about a Japanese adventurer named Naomi Uemura. He had just completed the first ever solo to the North Pole and he had done it with a dog team! I could hardly believe it! Over the years I had read many books about arctic expeditions from a hundred years ago or more, but I had no idea people were still driving dog teams around in the North. His story captured my imagination just the way listening to that radio show had when I was a young girl. As I read that story over and over, I began to wonder - could I do something like that? I had absolutely no idea how to run a dog team or where to go to learn how to run a dog team … but still… maybe …

A few days later while casually reading through the pages of the *Washington Post* newspaper I spotted an announcement that a local Siberian Husky Club was holding a meeting that very evening. I knew next to nothing about Siberian Huskies but from the books I had read I knew that they made good sled dogs. So I jumped in my car, drove to the meeting place, and quickly found my way to a room crowded with people happily talking about their dogs. I found an empty chair and sat down. The man next to me asked, "How many Siberian Huskies do you own?" "Well, none." He asked, "Why did you come to this meeting?" I told him about my dream to learn to run a dog team, figuring he would respond with something polite and move to another table. But he didn't! Instead he practically exploded with excitement!

"I know Natalie and Earl Norris!"

"Oh?" I said trying to look impressed. Their names meant nothing to me but I nodded and smiled as he continued.

"They live in Alaska!"

"Oh? That sounds interesting."

"They're world-renowned Siberian Husky breeders. I think sometimes they let people live with them to help with chores around their kennel. Maybe you could write to them and ask if they would let you come up there and maybe they might even teach you how to run a dog team!"

This seemed pretty far-fetched but I decided to keep listening. Trying not to sound too skeptical, I asked, "Do you happen to have their address?"

"Yes, I think I do!" he said as he yanked an address book out of his pocket and quickly thumbed through it. When he came to their names, he ripped out a blank page, wrote down the address, and handed me the jagged paper that read:

Earl Norris
Alaska

This kind man looked so pleased that he had been able to help me, so I nodded and said politely, "Thank you, this is very helpful."

Well, nothing ventured, nothing gained. That evening I sat down and composed a letter to Natalie and Earl Norris. I described myself as "a hard worker. I know nothing about dog mushing but am eager to come to Alaska and learn the sport." Truth be told, when I dropped the letter off at the Post Office, I figured it would never reach them with such a vague address and, even if it did, I assumed I would never hear anything back. But Fate seemed to be working again because about three weeks later a letter arrived from Natalie Norris telling me I was welcome to come to their kennel and spend the winter working as a handler. I read that letter over and over and over, making sure it really did say what I thought it said.

A handler. I had no idea what a handler did, I just knew that someone in Alaska was offering to let me live at their house where they had a bunch of sled dogs. That dream of riding on a dog sled was no longer just a dream; it was a real possibility!

Using a proper mailing address, I quickly sent a letter to Natalie thanking her and accepting her generous offer.

Jumping into such an adventure had not always been so easy for me. As a young girl I was extremely shy, easily controlled, and I found it very difficult to make decisions. But somewhere in the years of growing into adulthood I had blossomed into a person who made quick decisions and pretty much did whatever I felt like doing. I knew people often saw me as a little bit quirky, but I was now 34, and by this time in my life I could not care less what others thought. So I didn't bother offering much explanation when I gave notice at my house sitting and hospital jobs. I just told them I was moving to Alaska so I could learn to run a dog team.

CHAPTER 2

North to Alaska

On a hot August day, 1981, I loaded my few belongings into my trusty 1976 Chevy Nova and took off for Alaska. Money was tight so I planned on sleeping in my car and eating canned foods stored in the trunk. My companion was a German Shepherd/Collie mix named Amy. I was quite certain she would never pull a sled and I had no idea if the Norrises would appreciate my bringing her along, but she was my friend and I wasn't going to get rid of her.

Late in the afternoon of the fourth day we arrived in Sweet Grass, Montana and crossed the Canadian border into Alberta, Canada. The drive north through Calgary, Edmonton, and on to Dawson Creek was over a well-maintained, paved road and we made good time. The world-famous Alaska Highway begins at a round-about in Dawson Creek, British Columbia. From that point on, the word remote did not do justice to this road. Within a few miles it rapidly deteriorated into a narrow, winding, two-lane, gravel road paved with potholes. There were no ditches, trees grew right against the edge of the road, turn-outs were almost non-existent, and gas stations were even scarcer.

Four days later, on September 18, 1981, we crossed the U.S./Canadian border west of the small community of Beaver Creek, Yukon. I could hardly believe it! We were actually in Alaska! As I drove west, the scenery was breathtaking. A vastness spread out in front of us that was almost beyond belief. Flat tundra broken only by a few, rolling hills stretched across the wilderness for miles and miles ending in a distant line of beautiful, rugged, mountain peaks topped with gleaming, white snow. Exhausted after our 4,000 mile journey, we spent the night at Dead Man Campground.

The next day was my 35th birthday. After having lived for the past several days on canned goods, I decided to celebrate by splurging on breakfast in the cross-roads community of Tok. I was glad I had conserved my money because the meal was shockingly expensive. But the food tasted delicious and the portions were generous enough to leave me stuffed and still fill a large doggie-bag with leftovers for my lunch and of course to give Amy a special treat.

Late that evening I finally arrived in the tiny town of Willow, Alaska where Natalie and Earl Norris lived. At Mile Post 68 on the Parks Highway I saw a sign at the entrance to their driveway that declared the name of their homestead -The Howling Dog Farm. As I drove slowly down the driveway, a dog lot came into view. I got out of my car and stood looking bug-eyed at this incredible scene. Dogs, dogs, dogs! I had never seen so many dogs in one place. Norris's reddish/brown, two-story house faced north and in front of it were about 150 Siberian Huskies, each with their own dog house, all laid out in perfect rank and file. Off to the left were large pens with a couple litters of puppies running around happily playing. On the far right were about a dozen Canadian Eskimo dogs. A large pen set off slightly from the house held five very large pigs. To my eyes this was heaven on earth.

My arrival set off a commotion which brought Earl to the front door, so I walked over and introduced myself. After eight nights of sleeping in my car and nine days without a shower, I was pretty rough looking, but if Earl noticed my disheveled appearance, he didn't let on and seemed happy that I had arrived.

Over coffee Earl filled me in on a few things, "Natalie is in Norway lecturing and judging a Siberian Husky dog show. She'll be back in a week. There are three more handlers. Per from Norway, Claudia and Mike, they're both from West Germany. Claudia and Per arrive tomorrow. Mike's already here but he's off visiting some friends right now."

He showed me the bedroom that I would be sharing with Claudia and then, back downstairs over another cup of coffee, informed me, "Since you're the oldest and female, you'll be doing the cooking until Natalie gets back."

"Oh, … ah…well, okay," I said with a weak smile. I was afraid this might prove to be a tragic mistake as the most generous thing anyone can say about my cooking is that it is bland, unimaginative, and keeps you thin because no one ever asks for seconds. But I decided not to worry about it since I assumed we had all come to the Howling Dog Farm to learn about dog mushing, not to sample the cuisine.

The only sad thing was that Natalie's pet dog, Zeke, an Australian Shepherd, spent nights inside and, since Zeke was protective of his domain, this meant that my pet dog, Amy, was relegated to a dog house in the dog lot. For a couple of days she barked her indignation, but in time we both adapted to our new lifestyle.

Once all four of us handlers were in place, Earl wasted no time in putting everyone to work. After explaining the details of harnesses, ropes, and sleds, he assigned each of us a group of dogs to work with. My little group consisted of six Siberian Huskies; three were pure white, two were grey, and one pinto. We were also assigned a larger group of dogs to feed, water, and clean up after twice daily. First thing every morning we fed the dogs their breakfast, scooped poop, and then we would gather around the breakfast table drinking coffee and talking about which dogs we were going to train that day. Full of excitement, we would charge outside and hook up our teams.

If ever anyone thought dog mushing was a cruel sport they need only think of it from a dog's perspective. As anyone who has ever walked an untrained puppy on a leash can testify, dogs instinctively love to pull. Proof of this desire happened every morning the moment the dogs spotted us bringing our sleds and harnesses to the hook-up area. The entire dog lot would break into pandemonium with every dog running in circles around its house barking and barking, as if to say, "Pick me! Pick me!" The dogs selected for the team are led with a leash, head held high, a bounce in their step, and a huge doggie smile spread across their face. They are so eager to go that, while they are being harnessed, the sled must be securely anchored to an immovable object until the musher is ready to take off, otherwise, the dogs would leave on their own. Like their wolf ancestors, dogs naturally prefer living in packs. To a sled dog, mushing is the perfect sport because they get to pull a sled with a few of their best friends in the company of their favorite human. What more could a dog ask for?

Mike, Per, Claudia, and I were living our dreams of being dog mushers, so the Howling Dog Farm was a happy place for us handlers, too. In the beginning I drove a three-dog team. Every day was a new adventure. We would tear off down the curved forested trail, turn right at a fork, lope the team around a frozen lake, cross an open expanse of land, turn back onto Norris's trail and head for the dog lot where we received a raucous welcome from all the dogs that didn't get to go. Most of the dogs followed commands pretty well but the older dogs, those who were seven or eight years old, knew some tricks to play on novice dog mushers like me.

I remember the first time my leader decided to see who was boss. We were rocketing along the forested trail and came out on the edge of the lake where we were supposed to turn right.

"Gee," I called, telling my leader to turn right.

Apparently my leader decided she was going to be boss-dog that morning and made a sharp turn to the left.

I stomped my foot on the brake, stopping the sled, and called, "Gee! Gee!"

She kept lunging to the left.

"Did you hear me? Gee!" I yelled.

Team spirit took over and all three dogs started lunging left.

"Gee, you knuckleheads! Gee!"

With each lunge we were edging farther and farther to the left. By now the dogs knew who was in charge and it wasn't me. With one final tug, the U-turn was complete. I took my foot off the brake and let my lead dog have her way as we raced down the trail toward home.

Earl was cleaning the dog lot and looked surprised when he saw us approaching. The moment we stopped, he walked up and asked why we were back so soon. Earl was usually calm until something went wrong and then he could unleash his ire on you that was withering. When I explained what had happened, he glared at me and delivered a very pointed lecture on the fact that I was there to train the dogs, not the other way around. Thankfully the second team out that day was much better behaved and I was able to redeem myself.

After lunch we drank coffee and talked about our morning runs and then spent afternoons, seven days a week, doing what we called scooping-pooping.

In those first few days, we all were so busy during the day that we didn't have a lot of time to get to know each other as people. But as time went on and we gathered around the table for our evening meal, we talked about our lives before coming to the Howling Dog Farm. Claudia was maybe 18 years old and had come to Alaska for the adventure of running a dog team. She was very inquisitive about politics and the American health care system and could not understand why we didn't have universal health care in the United States. She did not enjoy my efforts in the kitchen. Mike was a gregarious, gentle-giant type of guy who never got upset about much of anything. Maybe in his mid-twenties, he had been a truck driver back in Germany. He loved the romance of the pioneer lifestyle and had a small piece of land up north of Willow where he was building a small cabin, relishing the task of doing it alone and with almost no money. I think Per was also 18. He spoke excellent English and was interested in going to college to study biology. A very kind and considerate young man, he often spoke about his home in Norway and always had lots of funny stories to tell. Night life in Willow was pretty much non-existent, so after dinner discussions wound down, we watched tv or read.

About a week later, Natalie came home. I offered to help with dinner but she smiled and politely declined, saying she was used to cooking by herself. I was only too happy to be relieved of that chore.

Natalie was small in stature, kindhearted, and had a gentle manner that made her very approachable. Almost every evening while Natalie prepared another scrumptious dinner, I would grill her with endless questions about dogs and mushing. I was impressed by her wealth of knowledge and even more impressed with her never-ending patience.

As the days passed and I got better at being a dog-boss, Earl assigned a few more dogs to me and I started running five-dog teams, then seven, then eight. Passion. Of all the times that I took a dog team out that winter, one run stands out in my memory more than any other. I planned the whole thing carefully and waited for conditions to be just right. It would be a rare after-dinner run. The sky had to be overcast, no moon, no wind, and the run would start well after sunset so it would be pitch black outside.

Finally, one dark, cold January evening everything was perfect. "Natalie, I'm going to take a small team out for a run." "Oh?" she replied, looking surprised. "Well, have fun."

All the dogs had been fed about two hours earlier and were not expecting to go for a run, so when I hooked up six white dogs and took off, the dog lot remained calm and quiet. In the beam of my headlamp, I could see the dogs were running well, but on such a dark night, when I turned my headlamp off, the white dogs became invisible against the white snow-covered trail. It was as if I were traveling on a magic carpet drawn by some invisible force that kept moving forward into the darkness, mile after mile. The night was totally silent except for the whisper of runners gliding over the snow and the dogs' steady breathing. It was peaceful and beautiful and exhilarating, all at the same time. It was the night I fell in love with dog mushing.

When I came back inside I told Natalie why I had made a run in the darkness and how magical it all felt. A warm, gentle smile slowly spread across her face as she nodded her approval. Then she looked through the window out into the darkness and a distant look came into her eyes. In that moment I think she was imagining herself out there running a team on that magical night. Passion.

Mostly our days were filled with routine but every once in a while we had a little excitement. Pigs. In a pen across from the dog lot lived five very large pigs. Natalie dumped all her kitchen food garbage, potato peels, gravy, left over vegetables, etc. into a bucket and Mike would dump it over the side of the fence so the pigs could enjoy their daily feast. Pigs are serious about eating and if the bucket of delicacies failed to arrive early enough for them, they would riot. They would bang into the fence, rocking it back and forth until they finally knocked it down and then went stampeding around the place looking for the bucket.

Five pigs running loose around the dog lot always sent the entire place into chaos with people shouting, dogs barking, everyone racing after the escapees, trying to get them back in their pen. Normally Earl and four handlers could have rounded them up without too much trouble were it not for Zeke. He was an Australian Shepherd and his strongest instinct was to herd animals through a gate. The problem was there was only one gate - the one at the end of the driveway, the one that led out onto the highway. Zeke would herd those pigs until he had them running full speed toward the gate.

It was usually Mike who tackled Zeke and dragged him into the house. With Zeke out of the picture, the pigs quickly slowed down and the rest of us were able to get them turned around and back inside their pen. Mike would come running with the bucket of garbage and dump it in the pig pen. All the pigs ever wanted was some garbage to root through so they never bothered trying to escape while Mike worked to put the fence back together.

CHAPTER 3
The 1982 Iditarod

Other than chasing pigs down the driveway, we occasionally watched a few dog races at the Montana Creek trails and every now and then went out to eat. But at The Howling Dog Farm pretty much nothing took precedence over training and scooping until March 6, 1982 when there came a great change. That was the day the Iditarod Sled Dog Race started. I had never heard of this race but apparently it was a big deal in Alaska because at breakfast Earl told us, "No one take out a team this morning. Get the scooping done so everyone can get back in the house before noon."

As ordered, we started scooping right after breakfast and then, just before noon, everyone put down their shovel and hurried into the house. We gathered around the table clutching steaming mugs of hot coffee while Natalie gave us handlers a quick summary of the race that was about to begin.

"The race starts out of Knik, that's a tiny village about 75 miles from here. This year fifty-four dog mushers have entered and they have teams of 12-18 dogs. They're going to race each other about 1,000 miles across Alaska to the gold mining town of Nome over on the Seward Peninsula."

"How are they going to get their food for such a long race?" asked Claudia.

"Before the race starts, each musher has to ship out dog food, people food, and other supplies to places called checkpoints along the race route. Racers have to stop at those checkpoints and show that their dogs are okay and they have all the required gear in their sled. Each musher has to have a sleeping bag, axe, snowshoes, camp stove, dog food, and booties for their dog's feet."

"What if a dog gets sick or injured?" asked Per.

"In that case, or if a dog is too tired to go on, the musher can drop the dog at any checkpoint and volunteers take care of the dog until it's flown to Anchorage where it goes to jail."

Everyone laughed and I asked, "What do you mean they go to jail?"

"When the dropped dogs arrive in Anchorage, they get sent to the Correction Facility in Eagle River, just a few miles outside of Anchorage where some of the inmates volunteer to care for them until the mushers can retrieve their dogs after the race. It's a privilege they have to earn through good behavior and they do a very good job."

Earl told us of some rules that protect the dogs and mushers. Every musher is required to take a 24 hour rest break at one checkpoint somewhere during the race. They can take it wherever they want and then they have to take another two hour rest at a checkpoint called White Mountain, near the end of the race. Each musher has their own way of resting their dogs along the trail to keep their spirits up because they don't want their dogs to get overly tired."

Natalie added, "There are volunteer veterinarians all along the race trail. Every dog is looked over at every checkpoint and the vets have the authority to remove any dog from the race at any time."

"What if a musher doesn't agree with the vet?' Mike asked.

"It doesn't matter, the vets have final authority."

For the rest of the day, into the evening, and every day for the rest of the race, we gathered around the table and listened to the hourly updates broadcast from radio station KABN. Of course we still had to squeeze in pooping scooping and short runs with the dogs but we never missed a broadcast. I was happy to learn that everyone competes equally. There is no women's division, no men's division, no senior class, no amateur class. Young, old, veterans, rookies, professional dog racers, and amateurs all run their teams down the same trail under the same rules.

As the race progressed and the radio announcer rattled off which musher had moved up and who had fallen back, Natalie and Earl would give each other a knowing smile and say things like, "Rick's making a move. Joe must be resting his team. Oh, oh, Dave dropped a dog. Susan must be taking her 24 hours."

I couldn't really appreciate the significance of these comments but the excitement at The Howling Dog Farm was contagious. Every day something happened that kept us glued to those hourly broadcasts and I soon found myself eager to hear the next story spun out by the announcer. "Today the trail was covered by a huge, fresh snowfall that buried parts of the trail. A bunch of leaders took a wrong turn and now there's a big furor over how well the trail was marked," the announcer proclaimed. A musher with the unlikely name of Babe led the pack into the town of McGrath and Emmitt Peters was fed a huge dinner for being first to reach some lodge. Sometimes a guy named Cowboy was in the lead, then Rick Swenson would pass him, then Susan Butcher would take the lead, only to be passed by Cowboy.

One of the most amazing things was how fast these teams were charging across Alaska. Then one day, as the lead teams were approaching the village checkpoint of Shaktoolik, the announcer said, "The race has been stopped! Mushers have run smack into a blizzard that is so powerful it swept some dogs right off their feet. No one wants to head out into this weather. Teams are holing up at checkpoints and villages all along the Iditarod Trail waiting for the storm to pass."

Earl and Natalie were stunned. "Must be some storm. This is the first time in its ten year history they have stopped the race."

When they broadcast the next update, we could hardly believe our ears, "Legendary Herbie Nayokpuk has decided to head out into the blizzard!"

Natalie gasped and shook her head in disbelief.

"Don't worry," Earl said with a wry smile. "That guy's tough as they come. Herbie's from the coast and he's used to that kind of weather. He'll be okay."

Herbie was from the small village of Shishmaref on the Seward Peninsula along the Bering Sea. This was his sixth Iditarod race. His teams were so fast and Herbie was so daring, he was known as The Shishmaref Cannonball. Talk about inspiring! Herbie Nayokpuk had undergone open heart surgery less than five months before the race and now he was heading out across the sea ice in a bid to put the storm between himself and the rest of the pack. If he could succeed, if Herbie could drive his team to the next checkpoint of Koyuk 35 miles away, he would be so far ahead of the other teams he would surely win the race. It was a bold move. But after spending around 24 hours battling 70 mile per hour gusts in blowing snow so dense he couldn't even see his lead dogs, the storm proved too powerful even for

Herbie. He finally turned back to wait out the storm with a bunch of other mushers in Shaktoolik.

That year, 1982, it took a little over 16 days for Rick Swenson to win his fourth Iditarod race. Susan Butcher, the only woman to finish the race that year, came in second, only three minutes and 43 seconds behind Swenson. Herbie Nayokpuk came in 12th. For me the most inspiring musher of all was Ralph Bradley. Early in the race Ralph had slipped far behind in the deep snow but he refused to give up and snow-shoed countless miles in front of his team along a trail buried under windblown snow. After 26 days, 13 hours, 59 minutes, and 59 seconds, Ralph Bradley proudly drove his team down Front Street into Nome. He came in last and, in my opinion, became a hero.

Over the past six months that I had lived at The Howling Dog Farm a steady stream of visitors had stopped by. Some were people who had worked as handlers and just wanted to have the experience of running a dog team, staying only a month before heading back home with grand stories to tell their friends. Several people from the past had trained and run the Iditarod. Some were big time racers like Iditarod champion Joe May. What impressed me the most was the shared love among all of us for dogs and dog mushing.

One thing became obvious to me - The Howling Dog Farm was a place where dreams take wing.

Dreams. I had never entered a race of any kind in my entire life. But listening to those race updates and all the exciting stories those visitors had to tell so inspired me that one dream completely captured my mind. Next winter I was going to run the Iditarod Sled Dog Race.

My cabin near Willow.

Jocko, number one lead dog.

Tommy, number two lead dog.

Amy, team dog and sometimes lead dog.

Bobby, team dog and sometimes lead dog.

Moose, team dog and wheel dog.

Sasha, team dog and swing dog.

Ernie, team dog and wheel dog.

Cletus, team dog, swing and lead dog.

Hank, team dog and wheel dog.

Ed, team dog and wheel dog.

Sammy, team dog.

Pam, musher.

Training the team around Willow.

CHAPTER 4
Getting My Team

The dream of every aspiring musher is to be standing on the back of a dog sled while a team of loyal and powerful huskies pulls them effortlessly along a beautiful, snowy trail. It all seems so idyllic when this movie plays on that screen inside your brain over and over and over. Of course it doesn't take long before you realize this is a sport that takes incredible devotion, much of your time, almost all of your money, and pretty much your entire heart.

At the Norrises I learned how to run a dog team, how to feed and water dogs, and keep them healthy no matter the weather. Experience and Natalie's coaching taught me how far they could run without getting overly tired. Best of all, the dogs I was responsible for training clearly seemed to like me as much as I liked them.

With spring approaching I began to make plans to get a place of my own. I got a job as a respiratory therapist at Providence Hospital in Anchorage working the night shift. Over the summer I spent my days off building a small 12' x 16' cabin across the highway from the Howling Dog Farm on the edge of a gravel pit. I squirreled away every spare nickel until I had enough to buy some dogs from Natalie and Earl and a few more from some other local mushers. I built each one a dog house, collected empty five-pound coffee cans from restaurants to use as watering cans, and got an empty five-gallon bucket from a construction site to use for the inevitable scooping. By August my kennel consisted of two Siberian Huskies, Bobby and Moose, four Alaskan huskies, Sammy, three brothers Ed, Hank, and Ernie, and my pet dog Amy who was a Collie/German Shepherd mix.

Every time I added a new dog I studied their personality with the idea that if I understood their likes and dislikes and what mattered to them, we could quickly come together as a team.

Long-legged Bobby was fast on the trail and a good worker; he liked the routine of training with the team but preferred basking alone in the sun. Moose was of course a big sort of goofy dog who was so strong I think he could have pulled me to Nome all by himself. Hank and Ed played together while Ernie seemed a bit of a loner. Only Sammy seemed to lack confidence but I figured with patience and some individual attention she would blossom. Amy was the only dog in my kennel that I had raised from a puppy and she had no lack of confidence. She never liked being tied up so as soon as I got home from work every morning, I turned her loose. Normally if a dog is turned loose everybody gets excited and barks at that dog, but there was something different about Amy. She had appointed herself top dog and would walk through the kennel, head held high as though she was the Queen of Sheba while every dog would step back and silently watch her pass by. Amy was a true alpha dog. Of course, I was the alpha person and what her highness didn't know was that she was soon going to get the chance to try out for a position as a sled dog in my team.

Even though it was summer, I fed my dream by purchasing a sled. I parked it right in front of my cabin and protected it from the sun with a blue tarp. Now I could look out the window and know that under that big, blue lump was my very own dog sled. There were vet bills for vaccinations, spaying and neutering, and the expense of materials to make harnesses and gang lines, but the single biggest drain on my bank account was dog food. Dogs can't work on corn flakes any more than I can. To be healthy and perform well, they need a diet of nutritious food and lots of it, so right from the get go I made the commitment to feed my dogs nothing but the highest quality dog food.

Because sled dogs love to eat, I decided to use that fact to build trust between them and me. I held the very firm idea that if the dogs were fed at regular times every morning and evening, they would learn to trust that their needs would always be met. I wanted them to believe that, no matter what, they could count on me, that I would always have their back.

I spent almost every waking hour preparing the dog's food, feeding them twice a day, hauling fresh water, scooping, playing with them, and talking to them about how we were going to run the Iditarod. Over the summer something happened to me that happens to a lot of novice mushers. Somewhere along the line I fell in love with my seven, furry, four-legged friends and we became a pack of eight.

Being smitten by a team of dogs was not unique to me. I noticed most mushers dressed in old, worn out clothes, seldom spent money eating out, and frequently displayed an inability to converse about anything other than dogs. However their dogs had the most beautiful harnesses, ate the best dog food, and, given a choice, these people generally chose to spend more time with their dogs than humans. There is so much love between mushers and their dogs that I believe dog lots are some of the happiest and most loving places on earth.

As fall approached and the temperatures began cooling off, reality started to set in. Money. I didn't have any, or at least not enough to acquire more dogs, prepare for the race and pay the $1049.00 Iditarod Sled Dog Race entry fee. Someone at work suggested I take out a loan. No way. I had worked ever since I was 15 years old, worked my way through college without borrowing money, and the idea of going into debt to run a dog race seemed ridiculous. Racing had never really appealed to me and I reminded myself that I had come to Alaska not to be a racer but to learn how to be a dog musher. My interests were and always had been in long distance arctic travel.

At this stage of my life I had faith in my physical ability but my main motivation for entering the race was to gain more experience in dog mushing before heading off to the Arctic. So after confronting the money issue, I hatched a new plan and trotted across the road to explain it to my neighbors, Bob and Robin Chlupach. "I'm going to run the Iditarod Trail but not the race. I'm going to take my dogs down to Knik, wait for all the racers to take off and then head out on my own. That way I can run the trail but I don't have to pay the entrance fee. What do you guys think?" Robin said, "I think that's a good plan." Bob just stared at me and made no comment.

Off I went to the Iditarod headquarters, which was then located in Wasilla upstairs over Teeland's General Store. Head volunteer Joanne Potts was sitting at her desk. I explained, "I'm a musher from over in Willow. I want to run my dogs down the Iditarod Trail but I don't want to enter the race. So I was wondering if you would please give me a list of the checkpoints so I'll know where to ship supplies." Silence. More silence. Then Joanne slowly turned her head a little to the left and, without taking her eyes off mine, replied, "Ahhh … I don't think so." There followed a fixed stare that told me I might just as well leave, so I did.

I wasn't sure what I was going to do at that point other than go on training my dogs. The biggest hurdle was the entrance fee, so I started picking up some overtime shifts at the hospital. When I had saved up enough for the fee I presented myself to Joanne Potts for the second time and said, "I would like to sign up for the race." Silence. For several seconds she just sat there staring at me. Then, almost in a whisper, she said, "The tenth woman." For the first time, a record ten women had signed up for the race and obviously this meant a lot to Joanne.

I forked over $1049 and the deed was done. I was now officially entered in the Iditarod Sled Dog Race, and even better, I felt no small measure of pride to be one of those ten women. Life got even busier but I did manage to have some human social life outside of work. A couple of times a week I visited Natalie and Earl and we would sit around the dining table drinking coffee while talking about dogs, and on other days I would amble over to visit Bob and Robin and talk dogs.

Bob had finished seventh in the 1982 Iditarod and had a wealth of information about the race. Over time Bob saw that I took good care of my dogs and he showed his confidence in me by offering to sell me a dog named Tommy. Bob asked a very reasonable price, so I put my money down and walked Tommy back to my cabin. Dog teams have a social order just like groups of people, so introducing a new dog can be a big deal causing a great commotion with everyone running in circles, barking and barking. But Tommy, brother to Dick and Harry, had such a casual, laid-back demeanor that when we walked down the path to my cabin, the other dogs just looked at him and made no fuss at all. Tommy turned out to be a hard working slob of a dog who loved to eat while drooling into his bowl. Since I still didn't have a leader, he became my de facto lead dog mostly because he didn't care where I put him in the team - lead, swing, wheel - it was all the same to Tommy as long as he got to run and eat.

Bob knew I was still looking for another dog and several days later told me about his dog Jocko. Jocko started life in J.P. Norris's kennel. (J.P. is Natalie and Earl's son and a sprint racer.) But Jocko wasn't fast enough for a sprint team, so he was sold to Bob. Bob was a serious long distance racer but Jocko wasn't fast enough for that team either. Bob thought Jocko would be fast enough for a rookie like me and he also thought Jocko might have some leadership potential, so I put my dwindling money down and walked back home with Jocko.

Jocko's entry into the dog lot was much more typical and caused the usual uproar. From talking with Bob I knew Jocko was a more sensitive dog than Tommy so my strategy was to act as though nothing exciting was happening and, without a word, hooked Jocko up to his dog house next to Tommy in hopes that he would make Jocko feel relaxed and welcome. It was a good plan and by day two they were standing nose to nose, tails wagging, pawing each other's shoulders, and making play bows, all the things dogs do when they're pals.

For the next two days I didn't hook up a team; I just set about studying Jocko's personality. Like people, dogs know when they have not measured up and Jocko knew he had failed twice to make the team. I could tell his self-confidence was low because he never made eye contact with me. I came to realize that Jocko was not the kind of dog who craved petting. He'd tolerate me standing beside him and petting his withers but he never wagged his tail or pressed up against my leg the way dogs do when they want you to stay beside them. That was his personality and I accepted him as he was.

Dog mushing is a sport where the musher stands on the back of a sled and a team of dogs are attached by lines to the front of the sled. There are no reins or leashes. The only control the musher has over the dogs is by using their voice to call commands. The most important dog in the team is the lead dog. Being a lead dog has nothing to do with dominance or size, it has everything to do with a dog being confident enough to run in front of a team of dogs, listen to the musher's commands, and follow them. The big question was whether or not Jocko could gain enough confident to become a leader. On day three when I started hooking up a team, every dog barked and ran in circles hoping to be chosen to go for a run. Jocko didn't look at me the way the other dogs did, he just stood beside his dog house barking. I needed Jocko to start feeling better about himself. I hooked him up in lead beside his buddy Tommy and put reliable Ernie in behind him and off the three of us went for a short run. He worked hard, kept his tug line taught, and proved he knew that "gee" meant turn right and "haw" meant turn left.

Every day after that I added another dog to the team until all nine dogs were in harness. Within a week Jocko and I were in sync with one another. He was a quick learner and within a couple of weeks he learned that "a little bit gee" meant to turn slightly right and "a little bit haw" meant turn slightly left. As the days passed, Jocko's confidence grew and soon he was making eye contact with me and he even started leaning against my leg and wagging his tail whenever I stopped to pet him.

CHAPTER 5
Training

When the first snow fell in October it was time to start serious training. I was still working nights, which was perfect because that gave me time during the day to train my team. Every evening I would leave my cabin around 9:30 p.m., hike the half mile out to my car parked beside the highway, drive 70 miles to the hospital, work all night, drive back to Willow, park, and hike back to my cabin, arriving by about 9 a.m. If I ever felt tired, that feeling melted away as I walked through the dog lot, petting and talking to the dogs who seemed so overjoyed to have me back that you would think I had been gone for a week. While the dogs bolted down their breakfast, I'd stuff down a bagel, gulp a cup of coffee, and head back outside to scoop. After my chores were finished and the dogs had digested their breakfast, I'd lay out the lines and harnesses and hook everybody up.

There was no way to get to any trails from my cabin without crossing railroad tracks or a busy road, so we would sled half a mile out to my car where I kept a small trailer with a dog box on it that had a compartment for each dog. I'd hook the trailer up to my car, load the dogs into the dog box, tie the sled on top of the box and drive about two miles to the Nancy Lake recreation area parking lot where there was an 8 ½ mile off-road loop.

It was a great place to train dogs and offered us endless opportunities to practice and learn to do things right. Straight out of the parking lot was a hill which gave us the perfect opportunity to practice sprinting uphill. The many, long, flat places were good for setting the pace and building endurance. Downhills were always slow to prevent jamming the dogs' joints. Since most local mushers used this trail, the dogs got plenty of practice passing teams going in the opposite direction without getting tangled.

By the time we got back to my cabin, I was worn out and ready to get some sleep. My goal was to fall into bed by noon because I would have to be back up by seven to feed the dogs by eight, followed by the inevitable scooping, and then head off to Anchorage for another night of work.

October started out with fairly mild temperatures and lots of snow but around mid-month there came a cold snap. I was so focused on training that I hadn't paid attention to just how cold it had gotten and neglected to start wearing my long johns. I also hadn't paid attention to the ever-expanding hole in the right knee of my jeans. One morning as we were coming down the last hill at the end of our run I spotted Bob Chlupach in the parking lot harnessing his team. I noticed Bob was bundled up head to toe in heavy winter clothing. Normally Bob was a very friendly guy but this morning, as we pulled up beside his team, he just stood there silently staring at the hole in my jeans.

"Hi, Bob!"

He looked at me, raised his eyebrows and, in a terse voice that suggested he thought I wasn't wired too tightly, said, "It's twenty below."

"Oh, I thought it felt a little cold today," I said, rubbing my knee which I now noticed was so red that it looked like an airport beacon.

Bob sighed, shook his head, and went back to harnessing his team.

It is amazing what your body can tolerate when you're young. Why my knee didn't freeze solid and snap off that winter, I'll never know, but I didn't want to get a reputation for being some kind of weird wilderness babe, so after that I started wearing my long johns.

Maybe part of the reason I was oblivious to the cold was how I lived. My tiny 12' X 16' cabin had a tiny wood-burning stove that was incapable of holding a fire for more than six hours. Every day after training I'd get a big fire going, patch a harness or maybe sweep the floor until it was toasty warm in the cabin and then I'd jump into my sleeping bag. When it was time to get up, the fire had long since gone out, the cabin was freezing cold, and more often than not my pillow was frozen to the wall. There was never enough time to get a fire going before I had to leave for work, so

I had grown used to dressing and doing chores in the cold. I never kept much water around since it would usually freeze solid but I kept enough in two big insulated jugs so that I could heat water on my Coleman stove to mix with the dog food and make a cup of coffee for myself. I seldom bothered with cooking and mostly dined on peanut butter and jam sandwiches. After all, I could get a warm, nutritious meal from the cafeteria at work.

By mid-November the cold weather had caused a thick layer of ice to form over the lakes around Willow and we were able to access a bunch more trails. I still had to haul the dogs but now it was only about half a mile to a different parking lot where we could sled down a hill and straight out onto frozen Nancy Lake. The lake is a little over two miles long and the trail went right down the middle. About half way across the lake both shorelines curved toward each other creating a narrows with very thin ice. At that spot someone always stuck a tree on either side of the trail to mark where the ice was thick enough to sled over, so as long as your lead dog went between the trees, you could avoid a cold dunking. Off the end of the lake was a vast trail system that could take you all the way to Nome. It was an excellent place to train my dogs for running long distances and giving Jocko a chance to hone his lead dog skills.

One day in particular stands out in my memory. It was a gorgeous, blue-sky day and Jocko was leading us across Nancy Lake when I saw in the distance another dog team on the trail heading toward us. On either side of us the snow was over three feet deep and the trail was like mushing in a long, narrow trench. As the on-coming team crossed over the narrows I could see it was a 16-dog team moving along at a pretty fast clip. Passing another team is always stressful because sometimes dogs will jump into the other team and create a tangled mess. I had no idea if this team would pass smoothly.

Many sled dogs refuse to leave a packed trail and jump into deep snow but clearly one of the teams was going to have to do just that. The team was less than 100 feet away and closing fast, when suddenly without a word from me, Jocko made his move. He lunged off the trail right into the deep, fluffy snow and led us in a big, sweeping arc past the other team. I swelled with pride when I looked back and saw the musher turn around and stand backwards on his runners so he could watch Jocko leading us, bounding through the snow and back onto the well-beaten trail. What a beautiful sight that was!

Jocko's willingness to go into deep snow was useful during that time because we were now training longer hours and I was getting less sleep. So, if it was a work night, we would sled until about eleven thirty and then I would command Jocko to turn "a little bit gee". He would dive off the trail no matter how deep the snow. Then I would call "haw" and he would turn a sharp left and bound back to the trail. Another "haw" and he would turn left and take us home. Jocko was becoming a very skilled leader.

Incredible, brilliant, talented - that was my Jocko.

CHAPTER 6
Bushes and Moose

One day when I got home from work I decided to leave Jocko home and put Tommy in lead of a small, five dog team. Tommy was emerging as a reliable number two lead dog and leading a small team would give him some low-stress experience. With such a small team I would also have a chance to help Amy learn to pay more attention to her job as a team dog. In the kennel she was self-appointed top-dog but in the team the other dogs treated her as just another dog. That didn't stop her from occasionally trying to take charge so she could do whatever she pleased.

I harnessed the dogs up with high hopes of having a productive run, but of course not everything always goes as expected. One of the ever-present hazards of dog mushing in Alaska are moose on the trail. They live in the forest and can weigh as much as 1200 pounds, surviving winter mostly on twigs and small tree branches. They do not take kindly to barking dogs and, if they get upset, a moose can seriously injury or even kill a dog with a single kick of its hoof.

With Tommy in single lead, Amy and Ernie behind him and Hank and Ed running right in front of the sled, we came off the far end of Nancy Lake and entered a heavily forested part of the trail. It was Amy who spotted the moose first about a hundred feet away off to our left. The moose glanced at us and then calmly resumed snacking on a willow. This was too exciting for Amy to pass up, so course she did what no proper, self-respecting sled dog should ever do - she started pulling us off the trail toward the moose!

"Amy! No! No! Gee!" I yelled.

I jammed the brake down with all my might. "Whoa!"

Ernie, never a killjoy, decided to join in the fun. "Ernie! No! No! Gee!"

Tommy was struggling valiantly, trying to keep us on the trail. "Gee Tommy, gee."

"Amy! No! Ernie! No!"

Hank and Ed glanced over at the moose. "Hank! No! Ed! No! Geeeeeee!"

The moose took off at a gallop. The dogs took off after the moose. Tommy was jerked off his feet and was being helplessly dragged through the snow! Everything was out of control!

"Whoa! Whoa!! We plowed through deeper and deeper snow. The dogs charged faster and faster racing through thick brush, whipping around trees, their tongues flapped like long red flags. The dogs were now in true hunting mode. Nothing was going to stop them from catching that moose!

Suddenly the moose stopped and spun around to face us! She raised her hackles, flattened her ears against the sides of her head, and angrily stomped her right, front hoof into the snow. She was ready for a fight!

The dogs stopped so quickly, the sled almost skidded into Hank and Ed. Heads down, the dogs closed in and tried to form a circle around the moose. The moose's head looked enormous towering over the dogs. Like a boxer, she kicked at Tommy's head with her hoof, then Amy, then Ernie.

With hooves kicking at their heads, the dogs now realized they had made one very big mistake and their hunting instincts completely vanished. Every time she flicked a hoof, the dogs backed up, until they were jammed against the sled in a tight knot. The moose moved forward, swinging her front legs left and right, kicking as though she were dancing in a chorus line! The dogs scrambled left trying to avoid the slashing hooves. The moose moved closer. In desperation, they lunged to the right straight into a bush. Bad mistake. In a heartbeat their lines tangled in the bush. They couldn't move! They were trapped!

The moose was furious. She lowered her head and gave a loud snort. She was going to attack my dogs!

Rage! I charged up in front of the dogs, threw my fists in the air, and yelled, "No! Nooo! Noooooo!"

The moose's head snapped back and she looked at me as if I were a space alien who had just appeared on the scene. "Go on!" I screamed. "GET OUT OF HERE!! GET OUT!!!" Luckily Miss Moose decided she'd had enough of my dog team. With one final snort, she whipped around and trotted away.

I didn't have time to think about the fact that I had just charged a moose with nothing but my fists and an angry voice. The only thing I wanted was to put distance between us and that moose in case she felt the need to come back for round two. The dog's lines were a tangled mess but I finally got them loose while snarling angry, mean words at Amy. With everything straightened out, we plowed back to the trail where I went eye to eye with Amy and gave her another, severe tongue lashing.

Only then did I notice Tommy standing on the trail with his head down. I wanted him to understand that I wasn't yelling at him and that what had happened wasn't his fault. So I walked up beside him, put my hand on his withers and talked softly, telling him over and over he was a good dog. When I felt his shoulders relax, we took off down the trail. Tommy did just fine for the rest of our run and got us safely home with no more drama.

November brought more changes to my team. I only had nine dogs and that seemed a little slim for a thousand mile race across Alaska, so I decided to approach Natalie.

"Natalie, would you be willing to lease me a dog for the Iditarod?"

"Yes," she replied.

"How much?"

"Enough to feed the dog for a year."

Sasha was a small, quiet Siberian Husky. She came from a very big kennel and was used to working with a lot of other dogs, so she blended in easily and became a good team dog. With ten dogs and me, we were now a pack of 11.

I really needed at least one more dog to make a team big enough for such a long race, but I was very low on funds and I wasn't sure what I was going to do. Bob to the rescue. A couple of days later I was visiting Bob and out of the clear blue he asked, "How would you like to borrow Cletus and use him in the race?"

"Really?" I asked incredulously. Bob smiled and nodded.

I knew Cletus was a strong, hardworking dog and he'd make an excellent addition to my team.

Just like that I had eleven dogs.

It was my day off when I took Cletus home. He was a big, yellow, long-legged, goofy, happy-go-lucky fellow who loved everyone. Dogs, like people, who come on too strong can be off-putting so, as we walked down the trail, I was a little concerned about how he was going to fit in. But I had a plan.

Part of my job was not just to study my dogs' personalities, but to try and understand what they want. One of the dogs in my kennel was a big guy named Ernie. We all have known people who are disliked by others, even though they are nice and try to fit in. Well, that seemed to be Ernie's fate. The other dogs tolerated him but for some reason they didn't like Ernie very much and almost never played with him. How would Cletus react to Ernie?

The entire kennel burst into the usual uproar when Cletus and I came within sight. I put Cletus at the dog house next to Ernie and walked away without saying a word. Later, I served the evening meal amid the usual barking and excitement and then went inside to read. After a few minutes I looked out the front window to check on the dogs and saw that everyone had quickly settled down and curled up inside their houses for the night - except Ernie and Cletus. Cletus was in a play bow with his front legs down flat on the snow and his behind in the air. Ernie was standing perfectly still with his mouth slightly open, looking at Cletus, tail wagging. It was as though Ernie was thinking *Wow! This guy actually wants to play with me.* From then on Ernie and Cletus were best pals.

All dog mushers can tell you stories about two dogs who were friends, who wanted to run together, eat together, even rest together. So it was with Ernie and Cletus. I almost always hooked them up side by side when we trained. On the rare occasion that I hooked them up beside someone else, they always glanced over at each other as if to say *See you after the run.* So, of course, I seldom separated them. On over-night training runs I always made certain they ate with their bowls side by side and picketed them so they could snuggle up together. Those two dogs and the friendship they formed is one of my happiest dog mushing memories.

My team was coming together nicely but I knew we had some challenges that wouldn't be easy to overcome. For maximum efficiency, mushers try to put together teams of dogs that are similar in size and run at the same speed and they often start the race with 16 to 18 dogs. My 11-dog team was pretty small by comparison and was made up of tall dogs, small dogs, fast dogs, and some not so fast, but that's what I had and there was not the tiniest doubt in my mind that those 11 dogs would be enough to get me to Nome.

But one problem remained. I had finally managed to scrape together enough money for dogs, dog food, equipment, and the entry fee, but I wasn't sure how I was going to get my hands on extra lines and snaps that I would need for the race. I gathered up my courage and went over to Willow Hardware, owned by entrepreneur and sometimes politician, Doyle Holmes.

"Doyle, I'm running the Iditarod this year."

"Oh?" he smiled and nodded.

"Would you be willing to sponsor me for lines and snaps?"

I had no idea what he might say, but he just smiled and nodded, "Sure. How much do you need?"

Just like that I had enough lines and snaps to get us to Nome.

CHAPTER 7

Becoming a Team

Happy dogs make happy dog teams. Like any good coach I wanted my little athletes happy so I mixed the dogs around in the team and took note of which dog liked running next to which dog. I studied each one carefully to learn their strengths and weaknesses, often switching dogs around so they could learn to be comfortable running in different positions. During December I started taking my team over to Norris's where we trained on their trails and sometimes headed north to Trapper Creek so the dogs could have different experiences. Every once in a while when Tommy and Ernie ran beside one another, Tommy could be mischievous and try to shove Ernie off the trail, but other than that, everyone got along nicely. Since Tommy loved working beside Jocko and was continuing to show leadership abilities, Tommy became my number two lead dog and Ernie moved back in the team where he happily ran beside Cletus. Even Amy mostly gave up on her endless shenanigans and became a somewhat respectable sled dog.

On Christmas day a bunch of us gathered at a friend's house. We were all mushers and had pledged that this would be one day when we would not talk about dogs. One by one people arrived with the usual smiles and happy greetings, filled their glasses with holiday cheer and found a place to sit. There followed a long, awkward silence, people looking at the floor, glancing up at the ceiling, shifting in their chairs. It was Dave who finally spoke up, "I can't think of anything to say." Everyone burst out laughing. Our lives were so filled with dogs and if we couldn't talk about them, we had no idea how to carry on a conversation. We spontaneously abandoned our no-talking-about-dogs pledge and spent the rest of the evening telling stories about dogs who made us laugh, dogs who made us mad, dogs who were emerging as leaders, dogs who performed amazing feats on the trail, and of course endless stories about puppies who were sure to grow up to be great sled dogs.

It was a loud and noisy crowd and the later it got the bigger and wilder the tales grew. But no one cared if we were exaggerating. We were happy because we were talking dogs and that was all that mattered. It was a very happy Christmas.

The next morning training continued. Every day while standing on the back of my dog sled I worked at developing a mindset that I thought necessary to run the race. *Keep alert, stay focused. Keep tabs on the dogs. Does someone have a leg over a line? Is a tail up signaling the dog needs tending to? Do they need booties? What's the weather like? How long have we been traveling since the last break? Am I cold, hungry, tired? Keep alert, stay focused.* Over and over in a cycle designed to prevent problems and keep everyone healthy and in good spirits. Always, always, always striving to be better. Learning to think ahead, to practice, to prepare, to do it.

To celebrate the start of the New Year I decided we would spend New Year's Eve camping out. The sun set somewhere around three o'clock in the afternoon and about two hours later as we glided down the slope and out onto Nancy Lake. The evening was calm, cold, and clear and I could see the pale light from a full moon lingering just below the black tree tops on the far horizon. In a few minutes the moonlight would dull the stars' lights but for now I could look up and see the Milky Way and stars so bright against the black, velvety sky it was impossible not to stand on the back on my sled and just stare at them.

The moment. The dogs knew the trail so I didn't have to call any commands. The only sounds were of the dogs breathing and the rasp of the sled runners against the crispy snow. We were alone in a black and white paradise. It was as though we had slipped silently into a state of grace, a state of total perfection. Something special, something magical happened out there on the lake that evening. No longer were we a pack of twelve. It was as though we blended together to become a single entity, as though we had passed through some invisible barrier. In that one moment we became a team.

Through January our training runs grew longer until some days we ran as much as 40 miles. We grew much stronger and tougher from the long hours. We had long since overcome most of our little idiosyncrasies. The dogs knew what to expect from me, I knew what to expect from them, and they knew what to expect from each other. Most of the time I was exhausted, but I was lucky because my supervisor at work, Darlene Jewell, was very supportive and scheduled me so that my days off were clustered together, giving me time to concentrate more intensely on training and catch up on some badly needed sleep.

January brought another opportunity. In the North, the month of January consists of long, cold nights and short, cold days so we started doing more training in the night to help the dogs and me gain confidence traveling in darkness. There are more risks traveling in the dark, but the more you push the edges, the more comfortable you become with risk. During these runs, I always wore a battery operated headlamp that looks like what coal miners wear on their helmets. When I flipped the light on, Jocko didn't seem bothered but the other dogs didn't like it. I could see it cast a shadow in front of them and prevented them from seeing where they were going to put their feet. At first they slowed way down and Sammy would start freaking out, dodging left then right as though trying to get away from her own shadow. So I turned it on for a few brief seconds whenever I needed to see. Training in the dark helped me learn to trust the dogs' instincts and rely on Jocko's leadership more than any other kind of training that we did.

February. Time seemed to be passing more and more quickly. I wished February had more days. I felt pressured all month working, trying to meet expenses with very little money and still keep up training. Like any family there were demands and time conflicts and some days I was too exhausted or busy with last minute tasks to take the dogs out. They clearly sensed my stress and were often very subdued when I came home from work. We were losing something and it was obvious I needed to get things back on track.

Happy hour. We didn't train; instead, every day I turned the dogs lose one at a time and ran all over the dog lot with them. These wild and crazy hours melted away a lot of my stress and the joy, the love, the passion bubbled right back up to the surface. We were happy once again.

By now I had burned through almost every dollar I had squirreled away but I still needed to get more dog food, more people food, and a bunch of other odds and ends. I had no idea what I was going to do. Big surprise. About that time one very generous fellow employee at Providence Hospital came to the rescue and donated a walrus tusk cribbage board to auction off. Suddenly I had enough money to buy almost everything I needed.

Yet another happy surprise came a few days later. Just as I was getting off work one morning the head of the employees association asked me to stop by her office. She explained, "The Employees' Association wants to do something to help sponsor you but they haven't decided exactly what that might be." She then handed me two banners, one for each side of my sled that said, "Employees of Providence Hospital".

"Would you be willing to put these banners on the sides of your sled?"

I smiled and said, "Of course. It would be an honor."

Over the winter, every day, I felt along each dog's spine and ribs to check their weight. This was important because I needed to be able to judge how much more each dog needed to eat to keep their weight and energy up when the temperature dropped low and, when it warmed up, how much less they should eat so they wouldn't get fat. This was particularly important where Tommy was concerned as he could eat more than any three dogs on the planet and outgrow his harness if I didn't keep an eye on his weight. Knowing how much to feed came in handy when I was trying to figure out how much dog food we would need for the race.

Food drops. That's what mushers send out to the checkpoints about a week before the race starts. During the race there would be 19 food drops, which took forever to prepare. The rules require each musher ship a minimum of two pounds of dog food per dog per day and one day's ration for the musher. Every musher spends hours and hours portioning, weighing and bagging dog food, preparing dog treats, people treats, people food, repair items, booties for the dogs' feet, batteries for your headlamp, and anything else you think you might possibly need on the trail.

We all used Coleman fuel to run our stoves but we didn't have to ship it because the Iditarod race committee provided it free at each resupply checkpoint.

Everything is placed in large burlap bags with the musher's name on the side for identification. These supplies are taken to a warehouse in Anchorage where everything is weighed in and shipped out. The mushers paid 10¢ per pound freight charge, which was a real bargain.

My shipment totaled 1100 pounds. With only my 1976 Chevy Nova to haul all this into Anchorage, I was in need of bigger transportation. Dave and Barbara Totten had driven up from California in their motor home to watch the race and were staying with Earl and Natalie, so I headed over to Norrises.

"Hi, Dave," I said as I sat down at the table with the inevitable cup of coffee. "Dave, I have to get my food drops into Anchorage tomorrow. Any chance you could haul them in with your motor home?"

"Well, maybe, but I don't want to overload my rig. The maximum weight it can carry is 1100 pounds."

"Great! That's exactly what my shipment comes to!"

Dave looked a little startled at my quick response and appeared a bit skeptical but nevertheless agreed to do me the favor. The next day I followed Dave into Anchorage in my car and together we unloaded the bags at a warehouse loading dock and Dave headed back to Willow.

I climbed up onto the dock and asked the guy doing the weighing, "Where should I put my bags?"

Without looking at me, he just waved his hand and, in a dismissive voice mumbled, "Over there."

"Okay, then what?"

"Sit down and wait!"

Never having done this before and thinking maybe I had accidently cut in line, I piled the bags up where he had pointed and sat down. He then proceeded to take the musher who had arrived after me and then the musher after him. When he started weighing in the third musher who had arrived after me, I walked over and asked, "When are you going to take my stuff?"

Apparently he had developed a hearing problem because he didn't answer and went on weighing supplies as though I didn't exist.

Enter Joanne Potts, Race Coordinator. Joanne was working at a desk on the other side of the warehouse and, unknown to me, had been watching this guy ignore me. I didn't know her very well but I was about to learn that Joanne Potts was someone you didn't mess with. She got up from her desk and walked straight over to the weigh-in guy.

"You will take Pam next!" she ordered.

Apparently this fellow was a little confused as to who was in charge because he pointed to the musher unloading his bags and asked, "What about that guy?"

Joanne extended her arm straight out, leaving about a half inch between the end of her finger and the end of his nose, glared directly into his eyes, and said in one of the most commanding voices I have ever heard, "She has been waiting patiently over 45 minutes! You will take Pam **now**!"

Mr. Hard-of-hearing-weigh-in-guy didn't look at me or say a word; he just started dragging my bags over to the scale. When he was finished, I paid the $110 freight charge and thanked Joanne for her courtesy. She simply took a deep breath, sighed, and shook her head.

The week before the race was very hectic. There was a mandatory meeting where the race marshal reads the rules and answers mushers' questions. Trail Manager Rick Hunter told us "the trail through Rainy Pass is rough, The Burn has no snow, the Yukon River is reportedly open in places, and Nome has no snow." After the meeting ended everyone milled around, discussing the implications of the news. I really didn't understand the significance of any of this and was standing off to one side by myself when Emmitt Peters approached me and said, "Hi, I'm Emmitt Peters," and shook my hand. I smiled shyly and introduced myself, "Hi, I'm Pam Flowers, rookie." He smiled and wished me luck. I could hardly believe he had bothered to take the time to introduce himself to me. Emmitt Peters, another legend, known as The Yukon Fox, had won the 1975 Iditarod, and placed in the top ten a total of six times. This would be his ninth race.

Mandatory vet inspections of all the dogs and running last minute errands occupied the rest of the week right up to Thursday evening before the start of the race when the Iditarod holds a big banquet where all the mushers and their friends and family gather. Natalie, Earl, Dave and Barbara Totten, and Kari Skogen came along with me.

Kari was working as a dog handler at the Howling Dog Farm that winter and she had volunteered to be my handler for the start of the race.

Dick Mackey was Master of Ceremonies and greeted each musher with enthusiasm as they climbed up onto the stage to be introduced and draw their starting number. Being a rookie with a very small team, I felt pretty nervous when my turn came.

Dick looked at me and asked, "Are you ready for the race?"

"Yes, I'll be coming up to the starting line with eleven dogs," I said.

Dick Mackey was a classy guy. There was no sarcasm, no sneer. He simply smiled politely, shook my hand, and said, "Eleven dogs. Good luck, Pam."

I dipped my hand into the mukluk (a fur boot) that Dick held up and pulled out a piece of paper with the number 43 on it. That meant my dogs and I would be the 43rd team to start the eleventh running of the Iditarod Sled Dog Race. Before the evening was over 68 mushers had dipped their hand into that mukluk and pulled out their number. There were 36 rookies, the most ever to enter the race. Even the first Iditarod race held in 1973 only had 34 entries, who were of course all rookies.

Friday was fairly calm as I went over all my gear for the umpteenth time and then hung around with the dogs, trying to relax and enjoy the sunny day. Natalie and Earl had volunteered to take us into Anchorage in their dog truck, so the evening before I tied my sled on top of their dog box and stuffed my gear in one of the empty dog compartments.

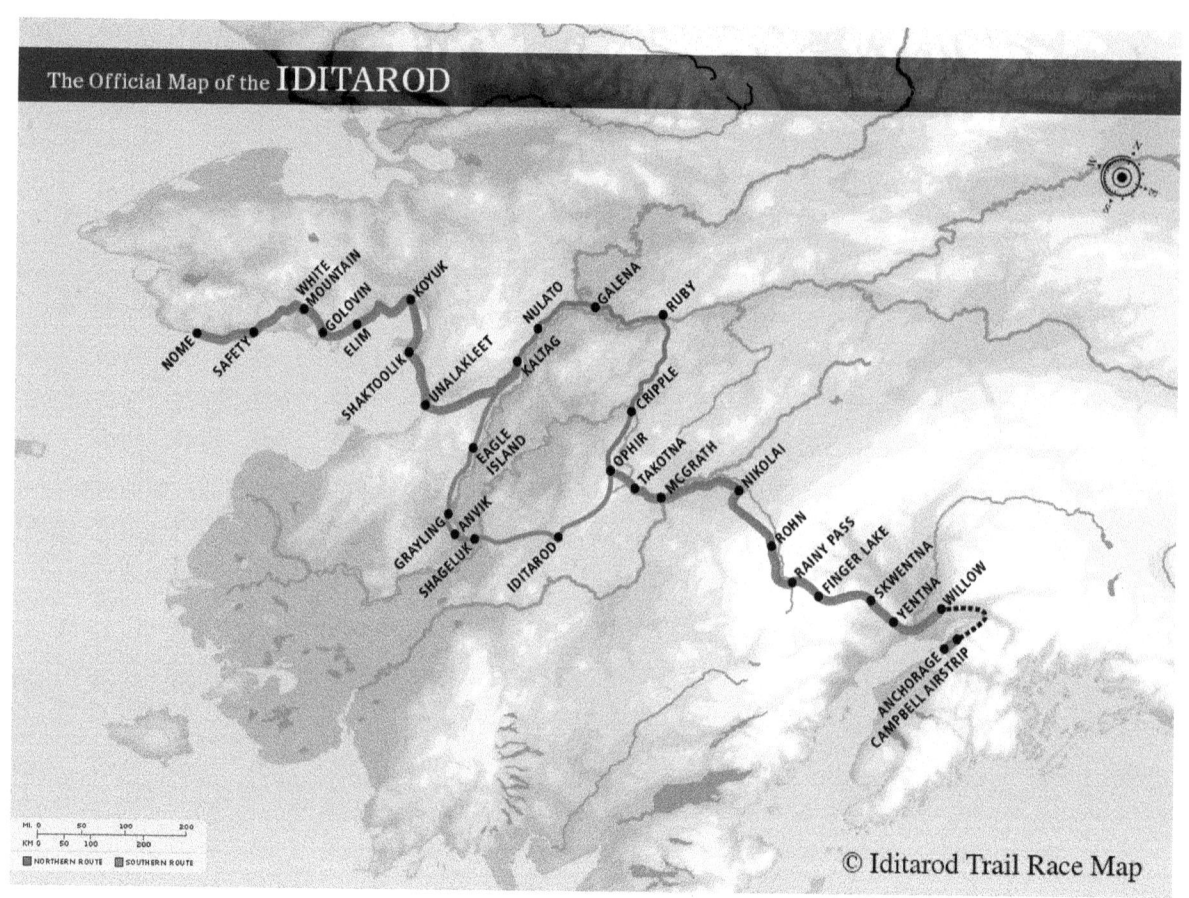

Map of the Iditarod Sled Dog Race.

Copyright and provided courtesy of the Iditarod Trail Committee.

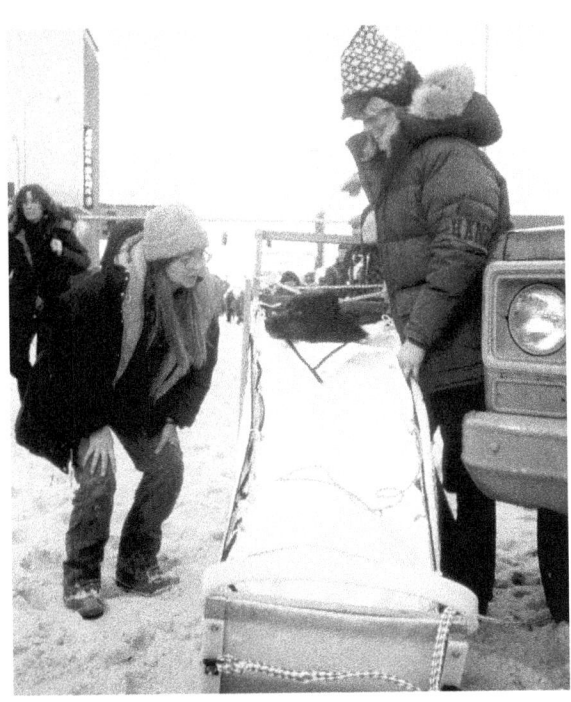

Pam and Kari check Sammy
before the start.

I'm excited as we come to the starting
line of the race.

Wearing bib #43, I walk along checking the team.
Earl Norris is petting Tommy.
Natalie Norris is wearing a light colored hat walking toward the sled.

My team starting the Iditarod Sled Dog Race on 4th Avenue in downtown Anchorage.

Teams resting at Rainy Pass Checkpoint.

Out of the Dalzell Gorge heading for Rohn.

Broken sled handle repaired at Rohn.

Coming onto The Burn where
there is no snow.

Tussocks cover much of The Burn.

Pausing for a break on the windy Burn
with little snow.

Abandoned safe at Iditarod checkpoint.

Teams resting at Kaltag checkpoint.

Tripods marking trail into Unalakleet.

35 mile long trail across Norton Sound from Shaktoolik to Koyuk.

Sledding along the north shore of Norton Sound.

Approaching Golovin.

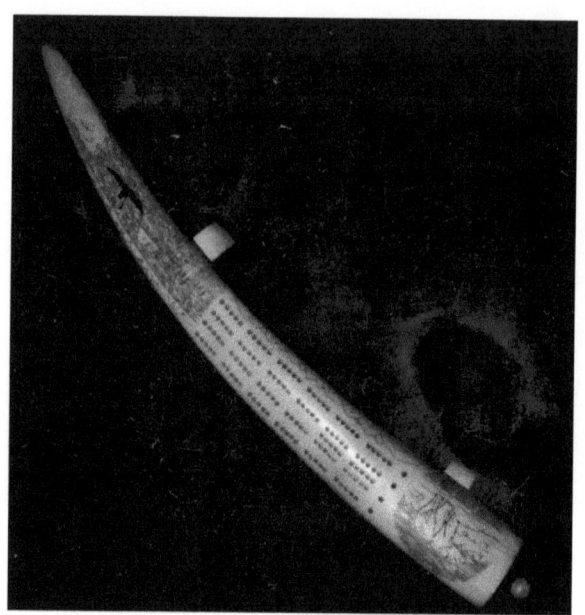

Walrus tusk cribbage board donated for auction.

Cake donated by Deborah Pugh for Providence Hospital employee bake sale.

CHAPTER 8

Race Day

Everyone was up early Saturday morning. We ate breakfast together, loaded up the dogs, piled into the truck, and headed into Anchorage. For the first time ever the race would be starting in downtown Anchorage right on 4th Avenue, a main thoroughfare that runs right through the middle of the city. Volunteers standing in front of temporary fencing guarded all the intersections that connected with 4th Avenue and waved dog trucks through to their parking space.

It was first come, first served. Earl pulled into a parking space behind another dog truck and we all piled out to start setting up. First Mike and Per hauled the sled off the top of the truck and then I attached the lines, while Kari and Earl attached short chains along the bottom edge of the dog truck to secure the dogs until it was time to harness them. Everyone lent a hand taking the dogs out of the truck and gently putting them down on the pavement where they could stretch out and look around.

When everything was as ready as it could be I took time to look at the scene. Wow! All night long, dozens and dozens of huge dump trucks had dumped hundreds of loads of snow on the street until there was a deep, well packed trail right down the middle of 4th Avenue! Thousands of spectators already lined the street behind the fencing, talking and pointing out mushers and dogs. People had even rented second story rooms from stores along the street and were perched on windowsills looking down at the festivities.

By the time all the mushers had arrived there were 1029 dogs standing along 4th Avenue, most of them barking.

While I checked everything over and over, Kari, who had volunteered to be my handler, stood beside my leaders Tommy and Jocko. Being a handler at the start of the race is both an honor and a huge responsibility. Because the race runs right through the city on main streets lined with spectators and goes through a bunch of intersections, most mushers leave the starting line with a trailer sled in tow. The handler rides the trailer sled. Two sleds help slow the dogs down and the handler is there to help if there are any mishaps with vehicles or spectators. The second sled and musher only travel to the first checkpoint. It's a coveted position and from the smile on Kari's face it was obvious she was pretty excited to be a part of the race.

Watching Jocko, I could see that he was nervous and looked a little withdrawn. I didn't want him spooked by all the hoopla. Bobby had been running in lead sometimes, so I decided rather than stress Jocko out at the start of the race, I would put him in swing, the position right behind the leaders, and put Bobby up beside Tommy. They had trained like that sometimes so I figured it's a good way to start and I thought they could handle the stress.

Everyone else looked bright-eyed and appeared to be enjoying the strange new sights - except Sammy. Cute, shy little Sammy loved being part of my dog team but she was not a party animal. She stood looking at the onlookers looking at her as though she was thinking, *I wish they'd go look at somebody else.* As a shy person myself, I could understand her discomfort.

"Natalie, Sammy looks pretty uncomfortable. What do you think I should do for her?"

"Put her in the basket. Lots of mushers do that with dogs like her. There's no rule against it and when you get to the restart, you can put her back in the team."

I tucked Sammy into the sled bag with her head out; she obviously felt better and I could see the stress fade away.

Honor and tradition. The Iditarod Sled Dog Race is steeped in Alaskan history and tradition. At 9:58 am the announcer called the name of the first musher to officially start the race. This is a ceremonial start honoring someone from the past who has made some significant contribution in mushing. This year's race was unique because the Iditarod Trail Committee had selected two mushers, Charles Evans and Edgar

Nollner. These two famous mushers had been part of the group of brave men who delivered serum in a relay across Alaska to Nome back in 1925 when an outbreak of diphtheria threatened the city. The efforts of those men saved the lives of many people and were well deserving of this special honor.

At precisely 10:00 am when the announcer called, "Go!" there is no team, no sled. It is only the spirit of Charles Evans and Edgar Nollner and the tradition they stood for that led the race down the trail.

Once the ceremonial start is complete, every two minutes over the next two hours and sixteen minutes, 68 teams will leave the starting line. Ten women and 58 men will compete across a thousand miles of wilderness, each one chasing a dream.

At precisely 10:02 am, the first of those mushers, Ken Hamm, left the starting line with 16 dogs and charged down 4th Avenue to the excited cheers of thousands of spectators. Following Ken two minutes later was Susan Butcher with 14 dogs. While we waited, people talked about the latest rumors concerning trail conditions and the weather. The temperature was 34°F and we all hoped it would cool off soon.

My starting number was 43 so when we heard the announcer call number 33 I looked at everyone and said, "Okay, we have twenty minutes so let's harness the dogs." Once the dogs are harnessed they know they're going somewhere and usually get excited. Maybe it was all the goings on but my dogs just stood there looking perfectly calm. Finally I heard the announcer call, "Pam Flowers, four minutes." That was the signal to start heading toward the starting line.

With butterflies in my stomach, I hopped on the sled runners while Earl, Natalie, Kari, and several volunteer handlers each grabbed the lines of two dogs and we started walking the team down the street. The dogs sensed the excitement and we started picking up speed. "Easy!" Everyone was gripping the lines as tightly as possible, trying not to slip, desperately holding back the dogs. "Easy!" The dogs slowed up some, but even so we arrived too soon. The team ahead of us still had several seconds before they could leave the starting line. The handlers skidded to a halt, braced themselves and struggled to keep the dogs from dragging them forward. Finally, the announcer shouted, "Go!" and the team ahead of us sped away.

"Next up, Pam Flowers." We moved up to the starting line as slowly as possible. Surprisingly the dogs settled down and stood quietly. "One minute." I got off the sled and walked along the team, calling each dog by name, stroking their shoulders, and checking that all the lines were straight and every harness just right.

"Thirty seconds," called the announcer. I stood beside Bobby and Tommy and looked along the team. Everything looked perfect.

"Fifteen seconds."

I walked back to the sled trying to stay calm, stepped on the runners, and looked back at Kari standing on the trailer sled. She looked happy and confident and gave me a quick nod indicating everything was okay.

"Three, two, one, go!" boomed the announcer's voice.

At precisely 11:26 am the handlers released their grip on the dogs.

"And they're off!"

CHAPTER 9
Anchorage to Eagle River

MARCH 5   **15 MILES**   **11 DOGS**

"All right let's go!" My team takes off running down 4th Avenue! My brain is spinning with all the excitement. *Wahoo! We're doing it! It's actually happening. We are running in the Iditarod Sled Dog Race!* The crowd cheers and claps. Of course they cheer for every team but right now they are cheering for us! I smile and wave. What a rush! I feel like a rock star!

We race along several blocks passing through I don't know how many intersections. Trail guards stop traffic; drivers honk their horns and wave as we go by. I smile and wave and smile and wave.

Rock star!

I am so proud of my dogs! They aren't bothered at all by the people or the city noise and confidently run through the streets of downtown Anchorage as if they did this every day. Somewhere along the way we make a right turn, dip down past a park, and onto a bike path. Yikes! There's a tunnel straight ahead! Nobody told us anything about a tunnel. *Just stay calm. Let the dogs keep going, don't think about it, don't step on the brake. Just keep going.* Whahoo! We zip right through the tunnel!

The last busy crossing is Tudor Road. The trail guards have already stopped traffic and I can clearly see on the other side of the road is a narrow cut through a snowbank just wide enough for us to sled through. Beyond that is a shallow ditch and then the trail leads into a forest. There's almost no snow on the road and as we cross I hear my sled runners grating on pavement.

If there's one thing Tommy loves, it's climbing up on top of things. Apparently he saw his chance for a little bit of fun because just as he and Bobby enter the cut, Tommy leaps up on top of the left side of the snowbank. The dogs on the left side of the team think this is a fun thing to do and one by one they all take their turn a-leaping! This causes the left runner of my sled to strike the snowbank at a sharp angle. The sled pitches over on its side. We crash, hard. My right hand rakes across the icy gravel in the bottom of the ditch as my chin smashes against the sled handle, giving myself what amounts to an uppercut.

The trail guards swing into action and grab the dogs before they can run off. They quickly help me right my sled. The blow to my chin has done a real number on my brain. As I stand up and look around, I can't figure out where I am or why I am standing beside a road with a bunch of people looking at me.

One of the guards peers into my eyes as though she is searching to see if I am in there and asks hesitantly, "Umm…are you okay?"

"Ah…I'm fine," I say, weaving slightly.

Actually I'm not fine at all. For a few seconds I stand there looking at my dogs, wondering what I am supposed to be doing. Tommy is looking back at me with a rather puzzled expression as though he is asking, "What are you doing back there?" Thankfully the dogs wait patiently, the fog clears, and I climb back on the runners. I manage to squeak, "All right," and we head down the forested trail.

My chin is throbbing. I press the back of my mitten against it and pull away a big glob of blood. In a matter of minutes my right hand becomes painfully swollen and nearly useless. So from that point on I become left handed and keep going. (After the race I will discover that a bone in the middle finger of my right hand was cracked and the knuckle will remain enlarged, permanently compromising the function in that hand.)

We come to a relatively flat, open place where trees don't crowd the trail and I hear a voice call from behind, "Hi!"

I look back and see the smiling face of Rick Swenson. "Hi," I call back. Champion musher Rick had drawn number 46 and so started six minutes after Kari and me.

"Mind if I pass?" he asks politely.

"Sure," I reply. Kari and I move the team to the right and tap our brakes to slow down. Actually, tapping the brake is not necessary because Rick's team moves past us so swiftly, it's as though we are going backwards. No wonder he has already won the race four times. (In 33 Iditarod races, Rick Swenson would go on to become a five-time Iditarod winner and finish among the top 20 mushers an astonishing 30 times.)

"Thanks," Rick calls as he sleds past. I wave and think, *Well, we won't be seeing him again.*

About two hours later we come to the first checkpoint at Eagle River where Earl and Natalie are waiting to greet us. I sign in and the checker counts my dogs and goes through the contents of my sled bag to make sure I have the required gear - snowshoes, shovel, axe, sleeping bag, booties for the dogs, food for the dogs and me, and a small package of ceremonial mail that each musher must carry to Nome. Only when the vet declares all my dogs fit and healthy will the checker release us to continue the race.

There is one problem I have to face. Even though Bobby is healthy and cleared to go, he is not doing well. He is such a loner and sits huddled up against my leg, looking downcast. I kneel beside him, "Having a rough time, aye, loner-boy? I understand. Let's see what I can do."

I hate to drop a dog so soon but all the stress and commotion had completely overwhelmed Bobby, so I tell the checker that I am dropping him. I walk over to Earl and Natalie and ask, "Bobby is really stressed out. Would you be willing to take him home?"

Natalie nods and says, "He doesn't look very happy. You're doing the right thing for him."

Earl loads Bobby into the dog truck and says, "He'll be okay. We'll take care of him until you get home."

We load the rest of the dogs into the dog truck and Natalie and Earl drive us to the next checkpoint of Settler's Bay. Why don't we keep going by dog team? It's impossible to sled to Settler's Bay because the route has to pass over the Matanuska River, which is never frozen. Of course there is a bridge and in 1973 during the first Iditarod race, mushers did drive their teams across the bridge. However, this resulted in total chaos for the mushers trying to sled north while vehicles were trying to drive south. After that mushers were never allowed to drive their teams across the bridge.

CHAPTER 10

Settler's Bay to Knik to Yentna to Skwentna

MARCH 5-6   55 MILES   10 DOGS

When we pull into Settler's Bay the scene is complete chaos. Mushers are supposed to leave in the order in which they have arrived at Eagle River but hundreds of vehicles clog the highway as thousands of spectators jockey for a place to watch the next part of the race. Because dozens of mushers are hopelessly stuck in the heavy traffic, it becomes first-come-first-leave. As soon as we get my sled unloaded and the dogs hooked up, the officials allow me to leave.

Jocko is now back up in lead with Tommy and my ten-dog team takes off looking very confident. The trail runs along a road through a well populated area with lots of side roads and driveway crossings, many with snow berms that are three or four feet high and nearly straight up and down. The dogs think all this up and down stuff is great fun and they could not care less that I am nearly bucked off at every berm.

As we pull into the checkpoint beside Knik Lake, there is a huge crowd of spectators hoping for their last chance to see the teams before we leave the road system and head into the forest. While I sign in with the checker the dogs sit calmly, resting - all except Tommy who is a born ham and loves attention. Tommy looks like people expect a sled dog to look, which makes him appealing to everyone with a camera.

"What's that dog's name?" a woman calls as she points at Tommy.

"That's Tommy. Just call his name and he'll look at you and smile."

Sure enough, for the next few minutes it's "Tommy, this way." "Tommy over here." Tommy's head looks like it's on a swivel as he turns this way and that, ears forward, pink tongue poking out between lips pulled back in what looks like a perfect doggie smile. Tommy obliges everyone as people laugh and snap dozens of pictures of his happy face.

I walk along the team checking lines and harnesses and when I get to Tommy, he cranes his neck back and gives a little "Woof". People laugh and more cameras click. The checker clears me to go. "Come on, Jocko. We need to get out of here before Tommy gets the big head." Ever the serious dog, Jocko leads us quickly across Knik Lake, up a hill, and into the forest where it's instantly much quieter after all the noise of spectators, snowmachines, and planes flying overhead. For the first time I feel as though we are finally on our way. The next few miles of trail are fairly straight, wide, and well-marked, so I try to convince myself to relax. But I'm a born worrier so I begin fretting about the infamous Nine-Mile Hill that is, you guessed it, nine miles down the trail.

Daylight is fading as we sled in and out of the forest, crossing swamps, creeks, roads, and soon darkness closes in around us. The trail slopes upward and twists back and forth seemingly forever. I know we have to be getting close to Nine-Mile Hill so I flip on my headlight and - "ACKKK!" - there it is, less than 100 feet in front of us! At the top of the hill, on the right side of the trail, on the very edge of the trail, sits a huge boulder. In that exact spot the trail makes a sharp, almost ninety degree turn to the right. Every year a few unlucky mushers catch a runner on that boulder, flip their sled over and, if they can't hang on, lose their team.

I bend my knees slightly, grit my teeth, and whisper to myself, "Hang on! Whatever you do, don't let go!"

There is nothing sled dogs love more than speeding around curves. In the beam of my headlamp they suddenly see their chance for a little unexpected fun. Instinctively I press down on the brake. Tommy and Jocko charge around the boulder and disappear from view. I press harder. In an instant Cletus and Moose vanish. Harder. As more dogs tear around the boulder, the towline angles over toward the boulder. It's happening so fast! I'm freaking out. *Don't crash into that stinkin' boulder!*

Somewhere inside my brain a voice shouts *Get your foot off the brake!*

In the last second I lift my foot and the sled slingshots around the boulder, missing it by less than an inch. "Whew!"

The trail drops steeply downhill and at the bottom where it levels out stands a checker with a clipboard. "Hi, Pam," he says with a big smile as he checks my name off the list.

I'm still a little freaked out by the near miss but I'm determined to look calm and collected, so I smile, wave, and say, "Hi! Nice night for a dog sled ride." He laughs and gives a little wave as my team and I speed down the trail. A few days later one unlucky musher will tell me that he flipped his sled and spent five, long, lonely, stressful hours walking the trail in pursuit of his runaway dogs. He finally found them snoozing alongside the trail, patiently waiting for him to catch up.

Making it up and over Nine-Mile Hill is not the only lucky thing that happens to my dogs and me. All along the first few miles of trail people have driven their snow-machines (that's Alaskan for snowmobile) in on side trails to cheer mushers as they pass by. But we haven't seen anyone in what seems like a long time and doubt slowly begins creeping into my brain. *A bunch of teams are ahead of us, so why is the trail so soft and mushy? Why are there so few dog footprints? Why are there no trail markers?* With my headlamp off in the darkness it seems that somehow I have managed to get off onto a side trail.

In one of our conversations before the race, Bob Chlupach had told me, "If you get lost, stop, turn around, and go back to where you know you know where you are. Figure out where you got lost and start again." I have no idea where we are but I'm certain we're on the wrong trail. For a few more minutes I anguish over whether or not to turn around and then finally decide there is no choice. I feel downcast as I mumble to myself, "We have to go back."

In the moment my foot is about to touch the brake something magical and completely unexpected happens. There, just a few feet ahead, on the left side of the trail stand a man, a woman, and a teenage boy not particularly well dressed to be out on a winter's night. As we pass directly in front of them, all three simultaneously raise a hand in slow motion, smile, and say in soft voices, "Good luck to you."

It is like seeing an apparition! I'm speechless. I look back, gawking at them for a few seconds and finally remember my manners. "Thank you!" I call, with a wave and a smile.

Who are these people? Why are they standing beside the trail in the dark so late at night? I'll never know but I am grateful to them because I know now that I am not lost, we are on the Iditarod Trail. It's late and with the stress gone, drowsiness sweeps over me like a warm blanket. We are sledding through a quiet place, so I pull over, check the dogs' feet, give everyone a snack, and we try to sleep. But teams pass by so often we really are not able to rest properly, so after about half an hour I get everyone up and we continue down the trail.

Sometime later it feels to me that once again we may not be on the trail so I flip on my headlamp. Bob had told me, "If you get off the trail, you'll just know." It's crazy how you can be on a trail you've never been on before, it's dark, you're bone tired and yet somehow you just know you are not on the right trail anymore. In the beam of my headlamp there are no dog footprints, no people standing around wishing me luck. All I see are snowmachine tracks on a very, narrow trail lined with dense forest. We sled up a hill and stop while I ponder our situation. *This isn't right. Apparently this time I really have managed to get us off the trail. We have to turn around and go back.*

There is no room to turn around but I trust Jocko. "Haw, Jocko, haw." As though he knows exactly what is needed, Jocko quickly turns left off the trail and heads straight into the forest, right into an awful tangle of dense brush and deep snow amid tall birch and spruce. Lines tangle among the alders and at one point threaten to hold us prisoner but one call to Jocko, "All right!" and he lunges forward. The other dogs follow his lead and we keep moving. About a hundred feet in I call "Haw," and "Haw" again. Jocko leads us in a huge, sweeping curve back to the mystery trail where we turn right. Thank goodness for all those training runs where we made big turns through deep snow to turn around and head back home.

It takes only a couple of minutes before I spot a little piece of orange survey tape hanging from a short tripod at the bottom of a small drop off into a swamp. I had missed that turn in the dark. I call "Haw." Jocko turns left and leads us back onto the Iditarod Trail. As I watch Jocko leading with pal Tommy by his side, I marvel at his confidence and amazing leadership ability. All those miles training, learning to trust one another, learning to seemingly read each other's minds is paying off. This does not happen running over the same trails day after day but by varying where we go, by exposing the dogs to new places and experiences, training on windy days and in the dark. It is a relationship acquired by working day after day for hours and hours with the same dogs and the same team. To be able to work with dogs on that level is a profound and gratifying experience.

A few minutes later in full darkness we bounce down a steep fifteen foot bank with multiple, short switchbacks and sled onto the mighty, frozen Susitna River. On the east bank is Susitna Station. It's not an official checkpoint but I see several teams parked so I decide to stop and go inside. The entire floor is carpeted with bodies of sleeping, snoring mushers. Back outside I heat water, soak dog food, and feed a meal to the dogs while I eat some Logan bread. I'll never get any sleep inside with all that racket, so I snuggle down into my sled bag and catch a bit of sleep.

Just before noon, March 6th, we pull into the checkpoint of Yentna Station Roadhouse. We have now traveled 70 miles. After going through the required procedures with the checkpoint person, I head inside the lodge and find it buzzing with mushers and spectators. Free food for mushers is on a table - spaghetti, fruit cocktail, Pilot Bread, Tang, and coffee. The roadhouse is run by Dan and Jean Gabryszak. They are dedicated and enthusiastic supporters of the race and treat every musher with kindness and provide a welcoming place to rest. I ask Jean if I can order a hamburger. She replies with a warm smile, "Yes, of course," and prepares a giant, juicy burger and fries.

The weather is perfect, around 10°F, when we take off and head down the Yentna River. It's broad daylight and, though some clouds move in and bring a few inches of snow, there is no chance of getting lost because the riverbanks tower over us by at least 70 feet. It's as though we are sledding in a canyon along a smooth and obvious trail. I can't see anyone in front of us or behind us; it's just me, the dogs, and the trail. For the first time since we started I am able to truly relax and enjoy the journey. I can see it in the dogs, too; Jocko with his shoulders relaxed and everyone moving along in a steady, easy gait. Some days standing on the back of a dog sled can be blissful, almost mesmerizing, and this is one of those days. It feels as though we could go on like this forever.

After a few more hours of easy sledding, up and down forested hills, past the mouth of the Skwentna River, we arrive at the Skwentna checkpoint, 104 miles into the race.

CHAPTER 11
Skwentna to Finger Lake

MARCH 6   34 MILES   10 DOGS

We pull in around 6:40, just as the sun is setting. What a sight! Up on the east bank of the river sits a two-story, log cabin belonging to Joe and Norma Delia. In the waning light I count thirteen teams scattered across the ice. Some dogs are sleeping, some eating, some casually watching their mushers cook their food. It looks like a staged scene out of a movie, calm and peaceful, almost gentle looking.

Checker Steve Johnson approaches, goes through my sled, counts my dogs, has me sign in, and then points to an empty spot on the river ice where I can park. It'll be dark soon so I rummage through my sled bag and find my headlamp. After taking everyone's harness off and checking feet, I walk over to where the shipped out musher bags are and quickly find mine. My right hand is still enormously swollen and looks like something you'd see on a cartoon character. It's a problem because I'm right handed, but so far I've been able to steer with my left hand and rest my right hand on the handlebar, using it only when absolutely necessary. The snowhook has been my biggest problem. To set the hook I drop it and use my boot to shove it deep into the snow. If the snow is firm I can never get it loose with my left hand, so I have to kick it loose and then pick it up with my left hand. Lugging buckets of water and dog food, booting, tending to just about anything is frustratingly slow and awkward. I decide to stay overnight and see if the swelling will go down by morning.

As I drag a bag back to my team I swing my gaze over my dogs. Jocko is sitting up studiously looking over at the other teams while Tommy, of course, is staring at the approaching food bag. Amy looks perky, tail wagging, as though she expects me to turn her loose so we can play. Only Sammy is curled up with her nose under her tail and seems disinterested in what's happening around her.

I go back and get a one-gallon can of Coleman fuel and fire up the stove. There is a hole chopped in the ice so I get out my five-gallon bucket and fill it half full of water, feeling grateful that I don't have to melt snow. Once the food is soaked to the point of being loose and mushy, I fill the dogs' bowls and hand out a dinner of warm, watery kibble followed by small chunks of ground beef. When every bowl is licked clean I take them up right away and store them safely inside the sled bag, otherwise the dogs will start chewing holes in them even though they are made of metal.

A quick walk up the hill brings me to the front door of the cabin. The place is packed with mushers talking and swapping stories. As a rookie I feel pretty shy so I just sit down and don't say anything. Ken Chase, one of the Iditarod legends for having competed in the first Iditarod in 1973 and every race since then, is polite and friendly. Scott Cameron, a rookie like me, is sitting by the stove chattering away, clearly excited to be in the race. I will see this again and again at checkpoints - champions, veterans, rookies, all mixing together, everyone feeling welcome and sharing endless, exaggerated stories about their dogs, laughing, and mulling over rumors about the trail ahead.

I don't want to take time away from this camaraderie to dig out my own food so I partake of the food provided by the Iditarod Trail Committee at every resupply check-point - spaghetti, fruit cocktail, Pilot Bread, coffee, and Tang. In the warmth of the cabin, it doesn't take long for everyone to start feeling drowsy, so gradually, one by one, we climb into our sleeping bags and within minutes the snoring begins.

I wake about five o'clock in the morning and decide to get an early start. The next checkpoint is Finger Lake but it isn't a food drop checkpoint, so I pack enough food into my sled to get us through to Rainy Pass, 64 miles up the trail. There is way too much food at Skwentna, so I take what's left and haul it back to where the drop bags are stacked. Anything left behind is shared with the volunteers at the checkpoints. Given how hard these people work to make the race possible, I am happy to have something to leave.

In the dusky light I count nine more teams that arrived after us during the night, creating a maze of trails going every which way. Somehow Jocko knows which trail to follow and leads us through the gauntlet of sleeping dogs. Amazingly, Tommy manages to ignore the smells of food lingering in the snow where several teams have eaten and already left. "Tommy, your nose must still be asleep." I get no reaction. "Good boy, Tommy."

The temperature is a pleasant -10°F and it's another glorious day as we head for Finger Lake. After a few miles the trail turns off the Skwentna River and runs across swamp after bumpy swamp. Just as we enter a forest the trail starts uphill and becomes one long twisting, narrow, snowmachine-chewed ribbon of soft, deep snow. We come to a fork in the trail but there is no marker indicating whether we should go left or right.

Then the unthinkable happens. Jocko and I have our first argument. Jocko decides we should go left but I think we should go right. Jocko lunges left. *Too late big guy, I have already decided we are going right.* "Gee, Jocko, gee." Jocko swings over to the right trail. "All right, let's go," I call. Jocko immediately swings back to the left. "Jocko, gee." Jocko swings right. "All right." Jocko swings back to the left.

Meanwhile Tommy just stands there looking completely disinterested, waiting patiently to see which way we are going to go.

Finally I get off the sled, waddle up through nearly waist deep snow, grab Jocko by the harness and drag him over to the right. I get back on the sled and call, "All right." Jocko swings left. Once again I get off the sled, waddle up to Jocko, and drag him over to the right. I bend over, put my face right next to his, point my finger and say through clenched teeth, "Jocko! *This* is the right trail!!!" Jocko flashes angry eyes up at me and then glares straight ahead. If ever there was a look on a dog's face that said "Okay, fine! But you're wrong!" it was on Jocko's face in that moment.

Back by the sled I say not a word; I just shove the sled forward and hop on. Jocko dutifully leads us down the right trail. Not to gloat, but this time I was right. Dogs aren't big on holding grudges so we quickly put our disagreement behind us. For the next several miles alders line swamp after swamp, spruce and birch cover the seemingly endless up and down hills that are more up than down. All day we don't see another team until we arrive at Finger Lake checkpoint around early evening. There are only six teams resting near the log cabin owned by Gene Leonhard, another Iditarod veteran. Gene is not home because he himself is somewhere out there ahead of us running the race this year. Someone comes out of the cabin and says to me, "You can go in if you want but there is no room, not even enough space to hang your harnesses up to dry."

I open the door and take one step inside. Sure enough the room is packed with people talking, laughing, and guzzling coffee. Harnesses smelling of wet dog, mitts and socks smelling of wet wool are hanging and dripping from every possible hook and line. It's steaming hot, looks like a sauna, and smells - well, trust me, it doesn't smell good. I decide not to add my own stinky self to the crowded room so I simply smile, raise my hand in greeting, say "Hi, everybody" and immediately step back outside.

How many teams are ahead of us I don't know but there must be more than forty. So much snow has been scooped up to melt for dog water that I have to make several trips into the forest to carefully select clean snow and haul it back. It's not hard, just time consuming. While the dog food is soaking, I check everyone over and am happy to see that they are in good shape. When dinner is served everyone wolfs their food down in true sled dog fashion except Sammy who only takes a couple of bites and then stuffs her nose under her tail. I worry that something is wrong with Sammy, so I decided to give her another thorough going over. I sit beside her and rub her neck and shoulders and then gently roll her over, massage her legs, check for dehydration, check her feet, and check for harness rub. I find nothing obviously wrong and she curls right back up again. I lay my sleeping bag out inside my sled bag, crawl in, and think about what to do. I started with only eleven dogs, the smallest team in the race, and now to drop another dog so soon will make it a real challenge to keep up with the other teams. I decide to wait until morning and hope Sammy will be feeling better.

It's a chilly night and I don't sleep well. Lots of mushers say that the next part of the trail is the most difficult and that it's best to set out early and travel in daylight, so around four a.m. I get up and make breakfast for the dogs. I'm relieved to see that Sammy has her appetite back and I am hoping she just had an off day yesterday. Two other mushers who arrived last night about four and a half hours after us are also up early. They are Steve Rieger with his 16-dog team and Ray Dronenburg with his 14 dogs. In the beams of our headlamps the three of us silently finish preparing for the day. At 5:45 a.m., about two hours before sunrise, I climb on the runners, call a quiet "All right" and off we go. Steve and Ray will leave a few minutes after us.

CHAPTER 12

Finger Lake to Rainy Pass

MARCH 8   **30 MILES**   **10 DOGS**

The snow heading out of Finger Lake continues soft and deep as we head up and down steep hills on a narrow trail lined with trees. Curves. Curves, curves, and more curves. The dogs of course charge full speed ahead, whipping around every curve as fast as possible. They are clearly having fun. Me? I just hang on and hope we don't have a close encounter with a tree.

About nine miles out we run along the side of a steep ravine, side-hilling on a trail that grows more and more narrow. To the left rises a near vertical wall that towers far above us. On the right side the land drops off almost straight down. As if this isn't scary enough, the sleds before us have gouged the right side of the trail as they sling-shot around a long, left-turning curve which has caused the sled-wide trail to slant down sharply to the right. As my sled starts to slough off the trail to the right, I try to lift it up on the left runner but I can't do it. The wheel dogs, Hank and Ed, freak out and dig their toes into the trail. If I don't do something fast the sled is going to slide off the trail and fall into the ravine!

I jam on the brake and call a halt. Even though there is an enticing curve ahead, the dogs actually stop. They all look down over the edge. I can see by their bugged out eyes, they sense our danger. I take a deep breath and step down off the trail. *Yikes this is scary!* It is so steep that the sled runners are now level with my head. *Stay calm. Work the problem.* I grab the right stanchion and shove the sled forward, which is sideways from where I am standing. The snow under my feet is deep and I start to flounder. I try desperately to hang on. I push the sled up with all my might and somehow manage to keep it on the trail.

In bad situations, dogs want people to tell them what to do. Every time I shove the sled forward, they move forward and the sled is almost jerked out of my hands. "Easy! Easy!" I call sharply. The dogs seem to sense the need to keep moving slowly. I keep moving sideways clutching the sled for dear life.

Inch by inch we move along the trail. We only stay like this for maybe a hundred feet but it seems endless. Finally, we come to a place where the trail broadens out just slightly and is once again horizontal with the earth. "Whew!" I climb up and get back on the runners. For a few seconds I lean my head down on the handlebar and thank my lucky stars that I have only ten dogs, any more and I might not have been able to pull this off. I raise my head and say "Good dogs. All right, let's go," and we move on down the trail.

We sled along a rim for a while and then turn sharply toward the edge. Suddenly the earth drops out from under us! Jocko and Tommy disappear from view, then Cletus and Moose. Two by two the dogs disappear down and around a corner. The sled whips around and suddenly I can see my team again.

The Steps! We're at the Happy River Steps! The place where whole teams fall off the trail and tumble down the mountainside. There is no time to think. "Hang on!" The dogs run full out down a long, long, narrow, steep slope at least 150 feet long. I'm barely in control! *Forget it, You got no control!* At the bottom of the slope there is a tiny flat spot where the trail twists sharply right in a near 180 degree turn. "Hang on!" We whip around and suddenly we are sledding, make that rocketing, down the second step heading in the opposite direction.

Echoing in my brain is the race marshal's command, "Don't use your brake on the Happy River Steps! You'll ruin the trail!"

I glance down between my feet. *Ruin the trail? What trail?* The middle of the trail is gone! There is nothing but a trench at least a foot deep. Obviously, mushers before me have jammed their brake into the trail in hopes of slowing down. *Don't worry about it, just hang on!*

Fear can cause irrational behavior. I jam my brake into the air beneath the sled. "We're not slowing down! Of course you're not slowing down you idiot! Air does not slow sleds! Just hang on!" A turn to the right and we are flying down the third step, hitting bump after bone-jarring bump. I glance to my left and see a terrifying, sheer drop off. "Yikes! Stay focused! Hang on!" My left hand is locked onto the handlebar with an iron grip and I feel like a rodeo rider on a bucking bronco. Suddenly, gloriously we are at the bottom of The Steps and zip along on the Happy River!

"Wahoo! Waaahooo! We did it!!!"

It would have been better if we had stopped and taken time to collect our wits, but we keep going. It is a rookie mistake.

It's only about a quarter of a mile down river until we turn right, sled up to a ledge and then start up Happy River Hill. When we reach a particularly steep slope, I jump off the sled and run alongside so the dogs don't have to haul me uphill. It's a long, hard pull. The dogs slow down and finally stop. I call, "All right!" and shove on the sled. The dogs give a wimpy tug and then just stand there. "All right!" Nothing. I walk up to Jocko and try to pull him forward. Nope, not happening. The dogs are as exhausted as I am after "The Steps" and they have decided they're taking a break.

Steve and Ray to the rescue!

I don't even notice that Steve Rieger and Ray Dronenberg have caught up with us and are patiently waiting behind me. They see my predicament and the next thing I know Steve is standing beside me with a gentle smile and asks, "Need a little help?"

It's embarrassing. With a weak smile and a nod, I say, "That would be great." Steve grabs the left side of the handlebar, Ray grabs the right and they start shoving the sled uphill. The dogs are startled when the sled suddenly begins moving, but they jump up and go to work while I trudge along behind. When the trail levels out a bit and we reach a spot wide enough for us to get over onto the side, Steve and Ray go back and retrieve their teams. I do my best to look cheerful as they sled past and shout, "Thank you!"

While we rest Leroy Shank and Mark Nordman pass us and of course both check to make sure we are okay. I assure them we are just resting. It doesn't take long before my dogs are back in the game and we take off again.

More miles, more ravines, more hills until finally, a little before noon, we come to Puntilla Lake and Rainy Pass Lodge. Most mushers have already left Rainy Pass more than 24 hours ago and there are now only ten teams here, all crowded along a hillside. But it's still a busy place. Small planes constantly flying in and out, mushers shuttling back and forth retrieving water from a hole in the lake ice, while others are walking dropped dogs over to the airstrip.

As the checker approaches I kneel down and check on Sammy. She looks away from me and stares off into the distance. I think she is more mentally than physically exhausted, so I tell the checker that I will be dropping her. The vet checks Sammy and finds her healthy but tired. The other dogs are declared to be in fine fettle.

Sammy and I walk over to the runway and I kneel down to have a little chat. "You're such a sweet, hard-working dog and I hate to say goodbye but I know this is the best thing for you." I stay with her for a while, telling her what a good dog she is, massaging her legs and shoulders. Separated from her team, I think she senses she's not going on with us and seems at peace with that. After a few minutes a volunteer comes over with a leash and leads her away. "Bye, Sammy." She doesn't look back but instead looks toward the small plane sitting on the runway. The man gently lifts her up into the plane, secures her in the back with a couple more dogs, and closes the door. The pilot revs up the engine, taxies down the runway, lifts off, and heads toward Anchorage. By this time tomorrow she'll be home. I wave and head back to my team.

CHAPTER 13
Rainy Pass to Rohn Roadhouse

MARCH 9   **40 MILES**   **9 DOGS**

The next terror on the trail is the Dalzell Gorge, better known as The Gorge. I want to run it in the daylight so we take off at first light.

At first we go steeply up and down but fairly quickly come out onto a vast open expanse and we are once again on the Happy River. Huge, six-foot, permanent wooden tripods mark the trail about every quarter mile. They are important because wind sweeps through here causing ground blizzards, often making it impossible to see the trail. There's no blizzard today but the wind is strong. A gust catches the sled and causes it to slew around, pulling the dogs to the left. At first they look back at me trying to figure out what is going on. We straighten out but then it happens again and again. But sled dogs adapt easily so they quickly get used to it and keep going. A couple of times powerful gusts cause the sled to slew so wildly that I have to struggle to hang on. All day I worry about whether I can handle the sled one-handed in The Gorge if it is as bad as people say.

The trail swings north and we climb up a ways, side-hilling along Pass Creek and up a steep climb to the 3,160 foot summit of Rainy Pass. There are willow bushes and rocky patches with very little snow on this nasty section but we make it through without mishap.

The earth starts to fall away to the right so I know we are approaching the entrance to The Gorge. Rumors claim it starts with a narrow, steep, twisting section of trail that runs along the side of a sheer drop-off that ends far below at a creek. It's supposed to be even more challenging than The Steps. Once again veterans' warnings echo in my mind. "The creek won't be frozen." "Bridge? Maybe." "Don't look down!" "Big hole, six foot drop!"

As we start moving gradually downhill I tell myself *people exaggerate, they like to scare rookies. It can't be that bad.*

Suddenly the trail narrows and becomes very steep. "Here we go!" Pain or no pain, I have to hang on with both hands. A few inches to the right the mountain plunges straight down into an open creek far below. *Tumble down there and we're dead!* The trail does not go straight down; it twists sharply left, right, left, and then right again. Sled dog delight! On each curve they jut their little dog faces forward and turn up the speed. Faster and faster.

"Whoa! Easy!"

Half way down there are so many boulders crowding the trail, there is barely room for the sled to pass through. The dogs are rocketing downhill as we swerve around yet another sharp curve. *We're going too fast! We're already out of control!*

"Easy! Easy!" I shout. Boulder! "Noooooo!" Too late. The sled strikes a boulder with an ugly thud and launches skyward.

We're going over the cliff!

The trail turns sharply left. The dogs take the curve. In just the exact right moment they jerk the sled right out of mid-air. Bam! The sled slams down onto the trail! Down and down we race. Several heart-stopping turns later, we arrive at the bottom of the gorge.

"Whew!"

The dogs finally slow their pace a little and I relax for, oh, maybe five seconds.

There it is! The bridge! *Yikes!* I can't believe what I'm seeing. The so-called bridge is nothing more than six, skinny, icy logs! They barely cross the ten foot gap over the creek.

We're supposed to cross on that thing??? Don't panic! Don't panic!

Hole in the ice? There is no ice! Six feet below us is a wide-open raging creek!

Okay, I see. I got it. From their angle the dogs can't even see the bridge. We're gonna speed up so fast they'll be across that stinkin' bridge before they know what happened.

A hundred feet to go. "All right! All right! All right!" I yell. The dogs hear the tension in my voice and start running.

Fifty feet! "All right! All right!" Faster! "Let's go! Let's go! Let's go!" Faster! Twenty feet, ten feet! The dogs race onto the bridge. Their feet slip on the slick logs. The logs start shifting under us! The bridge is collapsing!

"All right!!!" The dogs are running full out.

"We made it! We're across! Wahooo!" Thank goodness no one is watching as I yell and wave at the imaginary cheering crowd. "Thank you, thank you. Thank you very much."

We enter a slight curve just as I turn to look back over my shoulder at the bridge. Big mistake. **Crack!** The sled smashes into a tree and the impact throws me over the handlebar and onto the hard-packed trail. I scramble to my feet expecting to grab the sled as the dogs charge on. But they are just standing there looking at me. Then I see why. The handlebar is jammed against a tree and the dogs can't go anywhere. For a moment I feel relief and then I see it. The handlebar. The only thing I have to hang onto that keeps me from falling off the sled is broken in two pieces.

I am furious with myself. I fly into a rage stomping up and down the trail yelling, "How could you be so stupid? If you had been paying attention, this wouldn't have happened! .....Well? ..... What are you gonna do now?"

Just then another team crosses the bridge. "Oh, great!" When the musher sees us stopped in the middle of the trail he is not happy. "Sorry, broke my sled." As he maneuvers around us, he mutters something about me getting off the trail and keeps going. Obviously I would like to get out of the way but we're stuck in a tree. Anyway, there's no place to pull off.

I look at Jocko. He is staring at me as if he wants to know what we are doing.

"I have to fix this stupid sled." A quick jerk frees the handlebar. I take hold of Jocko's harness and lead the dogs along the trail until I find a wide place where we can get off the trail and won't be in anyone's way. I tie the team off to a tree and they lie down for a nap. After a quick search I find a branch about as thick as the handlebar, take out my tiny keyhole saw, and cut the branch off. With my teeth and left hand, I tear off a length of duct tape and use it to hold the branch in place. The tape barely sticks in the cold, but after several more applications I have a wobbly repair that's good enough to get us back on the trail.

About noon we arrive at Rohn Roadhouse. After checking in I move the team down past several other teams lining the trail and park them beside a big tree. Back at the checkpoint I ask the radio operator if he will get a message to Natalie and ask her to have a hockey stick and two hose clamps flown up to Rohn so I can make a better repair. Radio operators are all volunteers and provide a wonderful service getting parts, food, anything you want flown out.

The checkpoint is a nice, snug, well-built log cabin. Inside is a table with a few chairs, a blazing hot woodstove, and the usual musher stuff hanging around drying. Along the back wall two sleeping mushers occupy the bare, wooden platform that serves as a bunk. I have no way of knowing how long it will take to get the hockey stick, so the only thing to do is gobble down some spaghetti and fruit salad, enjoy the camaraderie, and wait. I'm pretty shy and don't talk much but it is fun listening to the other mushers swap stories.

While I'm resting and dozing beside the woodstove, a man comes in and announces, "Pam, one of your dogs is loose."

The vet accompanies me outside and, sure enough, standing in front of the door patiently waiting for me is Amy. At the sight of me she steps forward and wags her tail. She's not a dog to cause any problems but all dogs in the race must be secure at all times. I look down at her and smile, "Amy, I'm delighted you could come and join us, but I think we should go back and see how your teammates are doing." The vet bursts out laughing and heads back inside while I walk Amy over to the team. Upon examining her tug line, I see she decided to chew it through and come find me. She knows now that I'm nearby so, when I replace the line and hook her up again, she stays put.

A camera crew from a television station is there interviewing mushers from the back of the pack and the reporter asks me what I plan on doing when I get home. I tell him, "I'm going to soak in a hot tub, eat a box of bonbons, and buff my nails." He laughs and my lighthearted comment makes the evening news.

Amazingly the repair stuff arrives in about three hours! I take out my trusty, little keyhole saw, cut the hockey stick to a proper length and use the hose clamps to secure it in place. My sled is once again sturdy and trail worthy, so at about 5:30 in the evening we head out.

CHAPTER 14
Rohn Roadhouse to Nikolai Part 1

MARCH 9,10,11   75 MILES   9 DOGS

Not too far along we come out of the forest and onto the South Fork of the Kuskokwim River. It is a nasty, mile-long stretch of runner-ruining gravel with no snow interspersed with sandbars with no snow interspersed with random bits of glare ice. The wind is so strong it keeps blowing the sled sideways, pulling dogs along with it. Dozens of chunks of driftwood scattered about in inconvenient places stick up like gnarly wooden fingers waiting to snag any passing sled. It's nearly impossible to steer in the wind and the sled repeatedly slams into the driftwood causing it to bounce around and slew sideways, jerking the dogs around.

Almost as if to apologize for torturing us on the river, the trail becomes a nearly straight path through a beautiful forest. We are one of the slowest teams and I worry sometimes about keeping up but in places like this our pace picks up and I relax and enjoy myself. I know that somewhere up ahead lies the infamous Post River Glacier and of course veterans have warned me that this will be yet another nightmare. But I'm not so worried about it because I know from looking at a map someone showed me that it's really just a stream that freezes during the winter.

We emerge from the forest and the trail swings a hard right and goes straight for maybe a hundred feet. I can see across an open field that it quickly swings back to the left at almost 90 degrees and up a steep hill. "This is it, puppy-dogs. The glacier is dead ahead."

But wait… *what in the world?* Straight ahead of me, right at the sharp left turn, is a dog team in the bushes! Somehow they missed the left turn and plowed into the dense brush where they got stuck. The musher is wallowing around in soft, deep snow pulling on the leaders, trying to get his team back on the trail. He is clearly frustrated and upset with his predicament.

I stop my team and ask, "Would you like some help?"

"No!" comes a gruff reply "We're just taking a break."

He has managed to turn all fourteen dogs around but they are confused and floundering in the snow. The sled is still facing away from the trail and is firmly jammed against an unyielding clump of bushes. Every time the musher changes position to try and pull his leaders toward the trail he too tangles with a bush, trips, and falls over. He keeps pulling on his leaders but it is obviously hopeless.

I'm uncertain about what to do. The rules allow a musher to receive help when they or their team are in danger or out of control but he has refused my offer. Even so, I just can't leave them stuck and go off as though nothing is wrong. Finally, the musher stops, untangles himself from a bush, looks over his dilemma, and says with a deep sigh, "Okay, I guess I could use a little help."

I drop my snowhook and shove it deep into the hard-packed trail. Wallowing through the snow, I pick up the sled runners by the back end, and do my best to swivel it around the bush. It takes three tries, but I finally get the sled turned around and aimed toward the trail.

"Get on the sled!" he yells. "I am on the sled." "Step on the brake!" "I am on the brake!"

"Step harder!" "The snow is too deep. The brake is useless!"

By now he has gotten his two leaders up on the trail where they quickly turn right and start charging toward the hill. The dogs are moving; the sled is moving. The team is now beside the musher. I jump off the sled.

"Get off the sled!" he yells. "I am off the sled." He grabs the handlebar, hops on the runners, and heads up the hill without so much as a wave in my direction.

Thankfully, Jocko and team have stayed put, watching the craziness in silence. I decide it's time for a snack so we move over across the field near the base of the hill, well off the trail. There is no moon on this night and in the deepening darkness I feel drowsy after feeding the dogs and eating a chunk of Logan bread, so I decide we will rest here for a while. I take my boots off, spread my sleeping bag out inside the sled basket and crawl in. No sooner am I asleep than I hear a team breeze right past my sled. *Humm, that was close. I wonder why they are so far off the trail?* Then another team and then another. *Oh, well, at least they aren't running into the bushes.* Only later will I realize that by moving to our rest area we left a fresh scent across the field that will confuse some dogs who think they are on the trail, which explains why they passed by so closely. I guess it was another rookie mistake but the field was plenty wide enough for everyone and no harm was done.

It's very dark and late when another team cruises past. A few seconds later I'm jolted awake by a man's voice screaming in terror, "No! … No! … Nooo!"

What in the world?

"Nooooo!"

It sounds as if someone thinks they are going to die. I sit up and listen but I hear only dead silence. The glacier! Something terrible has happened on the glacier. I scramble out of my sleeping bag and run to the base of the hill.

"What in the world?" Charging straight down the hill toward me is a dog team! There is no sled, no musher, just a dog team! At first I don't know what to do. In the dark it looks like a lot of dogs and my first thought is to get out of the way. But very quickly I see it's not so many and I think I can stop them. In the middle of the trail I stand with legs apart, arms spread out trying to make myself look as big as possible. Luckily the dogs slow down and bunch up in front of me. They are wide-eyed and freaked out. They start bumping each other around and before I can even grab hold of a dog, they completely surround me. Low, threatening growls rumble from several throats. *Please God, please, please, please, don't let them start fighting.* Thankfully I see who the leader is and, even more thankfully, see it's a single leader with a double tug line. Together, we shuffle in a tight knot over to a big tree where I take one tug line off the single leader, put the line around the tree, and secure it back to the end of the leader's harness. It's not the best but it will have to do because all I can think of is that someone is injured or dead up on the glacier.

I take off running but just as I reach the bottom of the hill again I look up and see a headlamp bobbing toward me. *What the…?* Under it is a wide-eyed, young man, breathing heavily. He runs up to me and asks, "Did you see a dog team go by?"

"Yes, I did. I tied them off to a tree right over there."

"You tied them to a tree?!"

"Yes, don't worry, they're fine."

Over at the tree he sees how the dogs are secured and says, "Oh, okay I see what you did. That's fine."

"What happened?"

"Come on up and I'll show you."

"Okay, but I'm freezing. First, I have to get my boots and parka on."

At the top of the hill I get my first look at the infamous glacier. It is a sheet of glare ice that angles slightly down to the left and vanishes in the dark over what appears to be a cliff. Instead of crossing, the team had tried to turn left and follow what they thought was the trail. To the musher, in the dark, it would have looked as though they were going to drive over a cliff. No wonder he was screaming as though he thought they were going to die.

On the left where the ice begins, the musher's sled and two wheel dogs are tied off to a big tree. Apparently when the team turned left, they hit the tree with enough force to snap the gangline in two and freed the other nine dogs.

The musher leads the two dogs while I ease the sled back down to where the rest of his team is waiting. Fortunately he has extra lines so he quickly changes them out while I hold the sled. When he is ready to go, I suggest, "It's only an hour or so before dawn. Maybe you should wait and go then."

"No, no, no," he says adamantly, "I can't wait. I have to go. I have to get back on the trail right now."

The moment he takes off I dash over to my sled, yank my boots off, and climb into my sled. Unbelievably, as I am zipping up my sleeping bag, I hear his voice screaming, "No! … No!"

"Oh, for Pete's sake, not again." Then silence. I have seen the glacier and I know the silence means he has made it across, otherwise I would have heard the clatter of them going over the cliff. So I snuggle down into my sleeping bag and drift off for a few minutes of bliss.

CHAPTER 15
Rohn Roadhouse to Nikolai Part 2

MARCH 9,10,11   **75 MILES**   **9 DOGS**

The first light of dawn wakes me and for a couple of minutes I lie snuggled in my nice, warm cocoon listening to the total silence. But it's time to get up so I feed the dogs, grab another slice of Logan bread and walk over to see the cliff. It turns out that what looks like a cliff in the dark is really a steep, rocky, slope that is probably a small rapids in the summer. We head up the hill and across the glacier with no problems.

I am feeling really good about what my dogs and I have done so far. We've run The Gorge, made it down The Steps, and put The Glacier behind us, all without major mishap. But it doesn't take long before I'm jerked out of my reverie as the trail turns slightly to the right. As far as I can see there is no snow! Mile after mile we go, up and over hills, through forests, over runner-ruining rocks, across tundra covered with thousands of frozen tussocks, followed by more miles of forest and bone-jarring trail, all with no snow.

Finally, after I don't know how many hours, there is at least some snow on the trail as we emerge from the forest on the crest of a high, rounded hill. I call, "Whoa." The dogs stop as I climb off the sled and walk to the front of the team. "Wow! Would you look at that," I say softly under my breath. There it is, stretched out right in front of me - "The Burn". Yet another place that veteran mushers warned me about. "Miles of nothing." "Wind strong enough to blow you right off your sled." "Cold enough to freeze spit in midair." "Whatever you do, don't stop, don't camp, just keep going."

Before the race I read up on "The Burn" and learned its real name is The Farewell Burn. In 1978 the biggest forest fire in Alaska's history destroyed more than a million and a half acres of forest, creating a vast, open, wind-blown, prairie-like wilderness. As far as the eye can see there is nothing but snow-covered, rolling hills dotted with charred stumps and fallen trees scattered across the frozen landscape. It looks as though someone took a black marker and drew a wavy line through the jumbled devastation that stretches all the way to the horizon and vanishes among the distant hills. That line is the trail.

Off to the right I see the towering 20,320 foot summit of Denali, the highest mountain in North America. It is one giant chunk of granite. The sun shines down from a pale blue sky and bathes its massive white slopes with soft light. The vastness of this land is something to behold and it would be easy to feel overwhelmed, but I don't see it that way. To freeze such an enormous landscape, to push a mountain so high, to be in the midst of all this seemingly limitless power fills me with power. In this moment I believe beyond any doubt that we cannot fail in our quest to reach Nome.

A closer look reveals that much of the trail is clear of debris. I know this means that a volunteer crew came out ahead of the race and moved hundreds of fallen, burnt trees off the trail. Volunteer crews work hundreds of hours preparing the entire trail all the way to Nome. Without these generous, caring, hardworking people there would be no Iditarod.

I smile and say, "You know, puppy dogs, this doesn't look all that bad."

I climb back on the sled runners and call, "All right." The dogs move swiftly down the slope and out onto The Burn.

Occasionally a cold gust of wind crosses my face but for most of the day the temperature stays around a pleasant -12°F with a steady, light breeze out of the north. It's a gentle, beautiful, confidence building day. Around noon the wind picks up a little and loose snow scurries across the hard surface looking as though it's alive, like hundreds of tiny, little animals on the move. Late in the afternoon, with forty miles of The Burn behind us, we sled up and over a few more barren, rolling hills. All day one happy thought lingers gently in my brain, *With every minute that passes we are getting closer to Nome.*

Just after sunset a cold cell moves in and over the next four hours the temperature plummets to -30°F. Darkness makes the wind feel colder and I can feel the warmth slowly seeping out of my body. A sudden gust of wind hurls loose snow against my face, stinging my eyes. Then another gust and another and another until the entire right side of my face is plastered with icy snow. Freezing! I can feel my face freezing! I pay no attention to the trail as I try frantically to scrape the snow off with my mitten. Suddenly the sled lurches to a halt. I fumble with the switch on my headlamp. In the narrow beam of light I squint into the blowing snow, trying to see why we have stopped.

Jocko, my number one lead dog, turns his head and looks back at me. He is a decisive leader and I know he would only stop if he doesn't know what to do. I pull my parka hood forward to shield my face and walk up beside Jocko. His dilemma is immediately obvious. We are on top of a long, barren ridge and, right in front of Jocko, the trail splits in two. Both trails look evenly used.

Peering into the darkness, I can see no trail marker indicating which way to go, so I decide to leave the dogs and walk along the trail to see what I can find. I head down the left trail first with the wind steadily pushing me from behind, but after nearly a hundred yards I find no marker. When I turn around and head back toward the dogs, the wind blasts snow straight into my face. Every time I try to look ahead my eyes water and my eyelashes freeze together. I can feel my hands getting numb and my face beginning to freeze again. I raise my arms to protect my face but within seconds my arms feel numb half way up to my elbows. The wind is so powerful, every step is a struggle and I feel as though I'm smothering. I'm a little scared at how cold I'm getting so I try to quicken my pace.

When I finally get back to the dogs, they are all lying down with their backs to the wind and their noses tucked under their tails. Jocko raises his head and stares up at me with a look on his face that suggests he is expecting a decision. I'm so cold. All I do is stand there in a kind of stupor for what seems like forever staring at the two trails. My mind cannot make a decision. A gust of wind slams into me so hard it knocks me off my feet and the next thing I know I am on the ground looking straight into Jocko's eyes.

At long last the few brain cells that are not yet frozen generate a couple of rational thoughts.

You're getting hypothermic. Get out of this wind!

The dogs stand up as I stagger back to the sled and climb onto the runners. I call, "All right." There is nothing wimpy about Jocko or any of my dogs. As if he has read my mind, Jocko guides the team up between the two trails and with no command from me, stops when we are well clear of the fork.

The task of organizing my thoughts is daunting. *Get it together; stay focused. Get everyone out of the wind.* I walk up to Jocko, take hold of his harness and lead the team around to the lee side of the sled where they will be sheltered from the wind. Without my telling them, the dogs quickly bunch up into a little semi-circle and lay down. It is amazing how small a space nine dogs can fit into when they want to cuddle up. Tommy, number two lead dog and known for liking his comforts, somehow manages to jam himself right into the middle of the team where he will be the warmest. I climb over the dogs and sit down in the little space between the dogs and my sled.

It's a huge relief just to be out of the wind and I feel a strong desire to hunker down and go to sleep. *Stay awake. Work the problem.* I take a deep breath, stick my head up into the wind, reach into the sled bag, drag out my sleeping bag and stuff it under me. *Everyone needs food. Get the food bags.* I yank out a bag of dog treats, then my food, and last a thermos full of tea. I quickly cinch the sled bag closed so it won't fill up with blowing snow and hunker back down out of the wind. Just taking action helps me feel more in control.

Rule number one - dogs always eat first. When I look at the dogs, I burst out laughing. There are 18 bugged out eyes staring at that bulging bag of treats as though it is the last food on earth. But the drawstring on the treat bag is frozen and, try as I might, I cannot get it open. The only thing I can think of is to unzip my parka just enough to stuff the frozen lump inside and press it against my chest so the warmth will thaw it out.

"I know, I know, we're all hungry. Don't worry, they're worth the wait. These are the snacks with ground liver in them! Mmmm, yum, yum!"

After a few minutes I pull the bag out and go to work on the drawstring. My hands are stinging from the cold but, between using my fingers and teeth, I manage to loosen it enough to get the top open. I hand each dog a treat and am pleased there is no growling, no snatching, no me-first. Even gluttonous Tommy manages to restrain himself. Another round for the dogs and then I have to get some liquid and calories into me, too.

The whole time I'm gulping some luke-warm tea and wolfing down a slice of Logan bread, their eyes never leave the treat bag. "Wow, you guys made quick work of those treats. Okay, another round coming right up," I say laughing. Nine more treats vanish into salivating mouths. "I know there's no limit to what a sled dog can eat but don't you puppy dogs worry one tiny, little bit. We have plenty of food." Another round and then another and another.

Watching the dogs lick the snow in search of every last morsel, I realize I have made a rookie mistake. During the day I regularly rested and snacked the dogs but I had gone far too long without eating or drinking enough to take proper care of myself. If I had kept myself better hydrated, kept more calories on board, I wouldn't have gotten so cold so fast today and we might not be in this fix. Now here we are camped on The Burn. This is everything those mushers warned me about … freezing cold, strong wind, no place to camp. *Okay, take it easy. Think. Be logical. We have everything we need to survive … food, warmth, shelter, and each other. Keep everybody fed, stay out of the wind and you'll be just fine.*

About an hour later a musher drives up and takes the left fork. The wind is howling but he stops to ask, "Pam, are you okay?" I reply, "I'm fine. I don't know which fork to take so we're waiting for the wind to calm down." As he heads down the hill to the left he shouts back, "This is the right trail, Pam. This is the way." It's still very dark and windy and I see no reason to move, so I snuggle back inside my sleeping bag and drift off to sleep.

At around 1:30 in the morning Saul Paniptchuk pulls up and stops to ask, "Pam, are you okay." By now I am feeling rested and warm, so I climb partway out of my sleeping bag and say, "I'm fine but I can't figure out which fork to take so I'm resting here until daylight."

Saul looks at both forks and says with a calm, confident voice, "I'm taking whichever trail my lead dog takes," and off they go down the right fork. This is too good a chance to miss. The wind has died down some so I jump out of my sleeping bag, line the dogs out, and take off after Saul. His team is faster than mine and as dawn arrives

Saul pulls ahead and is soon out of sight. Once again we are alone enjoying another day of realizing my dream.

I would later learn that the left trail was created by five teams hunkered down behind the hill seeking shelter from the wind and brutal cold. They camped together and then sledded back to the Iditarod Trail, so we could have taken either fork.

The temperature rises to around -20°F and up ahead on a long open stretch I see a musher resting beside the trail. When we get closer, I realize it's the legendary Colonel Norman Vaughan. He is 79 and this is the sixth time he has entered the Iditarod. We stop and introduce ourselves and decide to travel together. We are still maybe 35-40 miles from Nikolai but, except for a few windblown places, the trail is in fine shape and we make good time, arriving in Nikolai a little after noon. The people are kind and helpful and friendly. I wish we could stay longer, but Steve Haver and Norman Vaughan are getting back on the trail so we all head for McGrath at about 5:00 in the evening.

CHAPTER 16
Nikolai to McGrath to Takotna to Ophir

MARCH 11, 12   54 MILES   9 DOGS

Although there are a lot of side trails to get off on, the run to McGrath is pretty easy. Steve Haver, Colonel Vaughan, and I travel convoy style with Steve usually in front. Jocko and Tommy have been running in lead a lot and they have done so much for the team, more than I ever expected, so this run offers a good chance to reward them for their hard work. I decide to move Amy and Cletus up to lead so Jocko and Tommy can relax back in the team. Neither Amy nor Cletus are experienced leaders but they are both smart dogs and I think they'll do okay. "Amy, you control freak, here's your chance to show us you can be a lead dog." When I put Amy up front she bounces around, wags her tail and looks up at me as though to say *I'm in lead! This is sooo exciting*! She is one proud, happy dog.

The second I put Cletus beside Amy, he decides it's playtime. "Cletus, I need you to help Amy. No goofing around, okay?"

We take off and they do fine for about five minutes and then Cletus starts leaning against Amy, trying to get her to play. "Cletus, knock it off." Being a leader is a big responsibility and requires a dog to focus and follow commands. I have to hand it to Amy, she rises to the occasion, ignores Cletus, and does better at following commands than I expect. In fact she goes about her new role with such determination, I believe I just might have a new lead dog. It is stressful for her though, and Cletus seems to sense this. He finally stops goofing around and helps her by following commands. I can see she is feeling the stress so we take an early rest break and I give her what she loves most in life - me stroking her neck and talking to her, one on one. "Hey, you lead dog, you. You're doing a pretty good job up here, you know. Especially since that reprobate Cletus stopped bugging you." At the sound of my voice, Cletus leans against my leg and wags his tail. "Cletus, you rascal, you're not doing so badly yourself."

Throughout the day we take lots of rest breaks and gradually lag farther and farther behind Steve and The Colonel, but that's okay. I am proud of Amy and Cletus for trying so hard and doing their jobs well. After a few hours I put Jocko and Tommy back up in lead and we soon catch up to Steve and Colonel Vaughan.

Maybe I'm imagining things, but for the rest of the day, watching Amy and Cletus working together back in the middle of the team, it seems to me that they're moving with their heads a little higher; like they know they did something to be proud of today.

All three teams pull into McGrath at about three in the morning and we are happy and grateful that our hosts are there to greet us. After the dogs are fed and bedded down we split up and sleep in clean beds for the night in homes provided by friendly, caring people who host mushers for nothing other than the joy that comes from helping a traveler find shelter and comfort on a cold and often challenging journey.

After enjoying lunch at the restaurant I take off first but Steve and The Colonel catch up and we travel easily in +5°F under a slightly overcast sky on a well-groomed snowmachine trail. This is gold mining country and along the way we pass a gold dredge frozen in the ice of the Kuskokwim River. These days gold is just under $400 an ounce, so I assume it's a money-making operation during the summer.

I didn't plan to stay long at the Takotna checkpoint but inside, standing behind a banquet table are half a dozen ladies all saying things like, "Would you like some pie?" "We have all flavors." "Freshly baked." "Best pies on the trail."

"No, thanks, I need to get going," I say with an apologetic smile.

"Oh, but you must have some pie." "Please sit down and have some pie."

They have obviously worked hard to bake these pies and their kindness is genuine and shows on their smiling faces, so I say, "Okay, sure. I'll have a piece." It turns out the pies of Takotna are so good, nobody can eat just one slice. After three, well okay make that four slices, I thank everyone profusely and waddle back to my team.

The temperature has warmed up to about 20°F and it looks like we might get some snow. It's a pretty nice run to Ophir along an old road but the first nine miles are uphill, so I use my foot to push against the trail and help the dogs, grateful for all those pie-calories that give me lots of energy. Steve, Ron Gould, Robert Gould, and I all arrive at about 10 p.m. The Colonel was also waylaid by the temptation of Takotna pies and arrives a little after midnight. It's so warm outside that once the dogs have eaten, they stretch out and sleep on their sides.

CHAPTER 17

Ophir to Iditarod

MARCH 13,14,15   **90** MILES   **9** DOGS

O phir is almost a ghost town. Surrounded by rolling hills with a view of dense forest, it was once a bustling gold mining community. These days it is now populated by moose, bears, wolves, lynx, spruce grouse, etc. etc. and two humans - Dick and Audra Forsgren. They are very kind and patient and help every musher within the race rules. Inside their home are eleven sleeping bodies, all grateful for a floor to spread out their sleeping bags and a warm room in which to have a snoring contest.

I enquire about the race and learn that three mushers have scratched, so the field is now down to 65 teams.

The next morning I wake up early. I don't feel like getting up but with the chorus of loud snores I'll never get back to sleep, so I drag myself up and out the door. The dogs have good appetites and scarf down their breakfast in typical sled dog fashion - that is they put their heads down and eat their food so fast I don't know how they have time to breathe. Then their tongues flick around scouring every inch of their bowls, seeking every molecule of food until there is nothing left but a shiny, empty bowl. They then sniff under their bowls in the snow for any morsel that might have gone astray. When they are satisfied nothing has escaped, they usually lie down and snooze for a while - except Tommy. He will stretch his legs to his neighbors' bowls left and right, snag them with his paw, and carefully inspect them for any leftover food. He never finds anything, but he always tries.

By around seven in the morning Jocko and Tommy lead the team back out onto the quiet trail. We sled alone along the road in the grey, early morning light, then turn left into the forest, cross a runway for small planes that doesn't look too well plowed, sled through a little more forest and then across the Innoko River. This is where the Iditarod trail splits. During odd years the trail goes west toward Iditarod over to Shageluk, up the Yukon River and on to Nome following what is called the Southern Route. During even years the trail heads north to Ruby, west and then south along the Yukon River and on to Nome on what is called the Northern Route. Using alternate routes includes more villages in this epic race and offers mushers different challenges. This is an odd year so we are running the Southern Route.

Much of the time The Colonel and I travel together and I learn a lot about him. He is an amazing man who worked as a dog musher on Admiral Byrd's 1928-1930 expedition in Antarctica and served in the Second World War. I soon learn that he loves coffee but hates setting up his stove on the trail. However, if I set up my stove and make coffee, he will regale me with endless stories. This is too good a chance to miss, so whenever we pause to rest the dogs, at the slightest often not too subtle suggestion "coffee would taste good right about now," I set up my stove, make coffee, and the Colonel rewards me with yet another amazing and entertaining story.

Turns out during WW2 his job was to dog sled to anyplace in Greenland where planes had crash landed and rescue the pilots. The planes were abandoned on the ice and, over several years, falling snow eventually buried them under several feet of snow. Colonel Vaughan is a man full of dreams and he believes he can locate the planes, bring them to the surface, and have some of them brought back to the United States to be placed in a museum. (By 1992 Colonel Vaughan would succeed at his Greenland dream, locating all eight downed planes and also helping recover one of the "Lost Squadron" aircraft. Colonel Norman Vaughan would also go on to complete the Iditarod for the fourth time in 1990 at age 84, making him the oldest person ever to finish the race.)

After sledding through soft snow and bad trail conditions, The Colonel and I arrive at Iditarod checkpoint Monday afternoon. We have been on the trail for ten days, so I decide to declare my mandatory 24 hour rest break. Dogs watch their human very closely and are amazingly perceptive. Somehow by the way I move my dogs know that we are taking a long break. I take everyone's harnesses off and start massaging their legs and shoulders. Ernie is last and when I finish with him I linger for a while on my knees, looking at my team. Bliss. Every dog is lying flat on their side under the warm sun unmoving, eyes closed, breathing. They are the perfect picture of total bliss.

Finally I get up and head over to the small cabin that serves as the checkpoint. Inside it is warm, steamy and crowded with harnesses, mittens, and socks hanging everywhere. We have been pretty lucky with the weather so everyone is happy and upbeat. A bunch of us sit around bragging about our dogs, telling tall tales of barely missed disasters and other suspect stories. There is a lot of laughter.

I'm surprised to learn that I'm the last musher to declare my 24 hour layover, but taking it at Iditarod turns out to be a very lucky decision. All along the entire race trail there is a vet at every checkpoint but there is only one medical doctor on the entire trail and he happens to be here at Iditarod. My right hand is still swollen and aches constantly. I can barely flex my fingers and I can't come close to making a fist. I'm starting to wonder if I'm doing the right thing by staying in the race, so during a quiet time I show the doctor my hand and ask his opinion.

He feels my fingers and asks me to try and make a fist. "Hmm… Well, your hand still has good color. If it starts to turn dark, scratch and get someplace fast so you can get help, otherwise you might lose your hand. So you have a clear choice, as long as the color stays good, what do you want more - to stop the pain or finish the race?"

Wow! He makes it seem so simple. I thank him for looking at my hand and go off by myself to ponder my situation. The part about - "you might lose your hand "- is kind of scary since getting out fast from who-knows-where might not be an option.

Afraid? I think back to something that happened to me when I was a 12 year old kid living in the Upper Peninsula of Michigan. I played clarinet in the school band and had stayed after dismissal for a music lesson. I was walking home alone in front of a row of houses when seemingly out of nowhere four boys surrounded me and began pelting me with snowballs. Those snowballs were hard-packed and they hurt. I swung the clarinet case trying to fend them off while they laughed and threw more snowballs. Suddenly an elderly man ran out of the nearest house, yelling, "Hey! Hey, you boys! Stop that! Go on, get out of here!"

He glared at them running away and then asked me, "Are you all right?"

"Yes, but I was really scared."

The man looked at me and said, "It's okay to be scared. You were trying to defend yourself. It's okay to be scared."

It was one of those moments everyone experiences in life when something happens that leaves a deep impression and changes how you think for the rest of your life. For me, those words - It's okay to be scared - changed how I think when I'm scared. They allow me to put fear aside and calmly think my way through scary situations.

I won't say I'm not at least a little scared right now about the possibility of losing my hand but my dogs and I have made it almost half way along the Iditarod trail and it doesn't make sense to quit because of what might happen. So, I make my decision - we are going to Nome.

Now it's time to see the local sights. Iditarod checkpoint, like the entire trail, has a fascinating history. Around the turn of the twentieth century gold was discovered in this area and it became known as the Innoko Mining Region. By 1906 hundreds of placer gold mines and thousands of gold miners were living in the vicinity seeking their fortunes. In 1908 someone discovered gold in this very place, which of course caused a stampede. By 1910 about 3,000 people lived in Iditarod, with another 7,000 people scattered throughout the region. There were several buildings, including a hotel, a bank, and all the usual businesses that make up a small town. Most people never found enough gold to even pay for their grubstake and by 1920 there were only 50 people remaining. Within two decades Iditarod was a ghost town.

I wander around exploring the relics of what used to be a town. Rotten boards stick up here and there, collapsed walls and floors, and the remains of the bank's concrete safe that once held a fortune in gold. The emptiness of the land speaks to just how few managed to eke out a living. The place has a very lonely feel to it, so I head back to the checkpoint cabin.

Another lucky break. The vet had overheard the doctor and me talking about my hand and offers me some crème that he uses for dog feet. "That will help take the swelling down," he explains. "Thanks, I'll give it a try."

Veterinarians play a very important role in the race. Sixteen volunteer vets are stationed at checkpoints along the trail this year, some serving at only one checkpoint, while others leapfrog ahead to work at multiple checkpoints as the race moves along. At every checkpoint every dog is looked at by a vet. They are a tremendously important asset to the mushers who often consult with them about whether or not to drop a dog. Usually it's the musher who decides a dog needs to be dropped, but it's often a joint decision between musher and vet. But always it's the vet who has the final say-so about whether a dog or even an entire team can continue in the race.

During the day Cletus and Ernie play a little with one another but mostly my dogs watch with only casual interest as four teams arrive and a few leave. After dark we all sit around a small, brown square-shaped oil stove that keeps the cabin toasty warm, drink coffee, eat, and tell shamelessly exaggerated stories about our dogs. When we decide to call it a night, a bunch of mushers, me included, place our mitts on top of the stove to dry out overnight. About an hour after lights out someone yells "Fire!" I roll over and see flames shooting up from the top of the stove and the room quickly fills with the stench of burning wool and melting polyester. Without my glasses on it is hard to tell who is being the hero but somehow someone manages to throw the blazing pile of mitts out into the snow. There doesn't seem to be any point in getting up, so everyone goes back to sleep. Within seconds loud snoring rattles the cabin walls.

In the morning I am amazed and happy to see that the swelling in my hand has gone way down and my fingers are a lot more flexible. By 10 a.m. everyone has left but I can't leave for another four hours. The two men running the checkpoint are concerned about how far behind the pack I am going to be. When the time comes to leave, they are standing right there with a clipboard ready for me to sign so I don't spend even one second longer here than required. I appreciate their consideration and at 2:10 p.m., March 15, I lift my snowhook, wave good bye and head out.

CHAPTER 18
Iditarod to Shageluk to Anvik to Grayling

MARCH 15, 16, 17   **65 MILES PLUS 25 MILES PLUS 18**   **9 DOGS**

The trail to Shageluk is quite nice, though a bit narrow in places. The trauma merchants had told me that the biggest challenge of this part of the trail was going up and down hill after hill after hill and that it would wear out my dogs. There are lots of hills, no denying that, but the dogs are well rested and we have no problems. For a while I move Jocko back in the team and move Amy up beside Tommy where she puts in another good showing. In a few hours we catch up to Scott Cameron who is resting his team beside the trail. I stop to visit and once again he impresses me with his enthusiasm. He seems completely captivated by the fact that he is actually running his dog team over the Iditarod Trail. The reality of the Iditarod Sled Dog Race is that most mushers have no illusions about winning, we simply seek the grace and beauty of being on the trail with our dogs, watching them do what they love.

My dogs are feeling pretty spunky and we make good time. After sleeping part of the night on the trail, we get into Shageluk around 10:00 a.m. March 16. Hamilton E. Hamilton, a legend in his own right for his dedication to the race, checks us in. He tells me the field is getting smaller because he heard a report that more teams have scratched. As of now a total of eight mushers have scratched, leaving 60 scattered along the trail. The dogs are doing well and I am determined to catch up with the pack, so we stay just four hours and head right back out.

In between hills is a mix of lakes and swamps and sloughs but overall sledding is not bad. We arrive at the mighty Yukon River, another milestone in our quest to reach Nome. We cross to the other side and climb up a steep bank. From there it's an easy drive down a road to the Anvik community center and again we only stay for a brief rest before taking off for Grayling, just 18 miles up the Yukon River.

It's just after midnight and very quiet as we pull up to the Grayling community center. What a relief! I count six teams lined out resting, which means we have finally caught up. While the checker goes through my mandatory gear and signs me in, only one musher is out tending to his team and that is Colonel Norman Vaughan. Once again I am impressed by this amazing man. He is lying on his left side, propped up on his elbow next to his team pulling himself along using his right hand to massage his dogs' legs and shoulders. When he sees me a huge smile lights up his face as he shouts, "Pam! Is that you?" "It's me," I say with a big, happy smile. "You're game. You are game!" he says with enthusiasm.

My dogs and I had worked hard to get here and those words make for a very proud moment.

Even though my dogs are tired they eat well and quickly curl up to sleep the night away. By the time all my chores are finished it's 2:30 in the morning and I'm so sleepy I can hardly stand up, so I finally stagger off to the community center for some badly needed rest.

CHAPTER 19
Grayling to Eagle Island

MARCH 17, 18   60 MILES   9 DOGS

I'm up after only four hours of sleep and go out to look at my dogs. Scott Cameron's team is resting nicely and four other teams are in various stages of preparation for their departure. For having gotten so little sleep, I'm feeling pretty good and I'm happy to see that my dogs are wide awake watching the activities. When they see me coming toward them, all nine stand up as though they're thinking we're going to leave, too, but we've been traveling fairly hard, so I decide we will stay a little bit longer and leave about mid-morning. In the meantime breakfasts are gobbled down and bowls are licked clean.

I decide to spend a little time cleaning out my sled bag, mainly to see how many booties are left. I had spent a lot of time during the summer working with a cranky, used sewing machine and had managed to produce several hundred booties. They are made of bunting material and held in place around a dog's ankle with Velcro. When snow is coarse and abrasive, whether during training or on the race trail, dogs wear booties to protect their feet and mushers are required to have an adequate supply of them in their sled at all times. Because we have had warm temperatures during most of the race, the snow has been soft and I haven't had to put booties on my dogs very often, so I am happy that find there is still a nice supply left.

The dogs are full of energy as we head out around 10:00 a.m. Five teams have set out before us so we travel alone for several miles. Heading up the Yukon is so different from what we have sledded over so far. There is a constant head wind that shifts the snow around, often covering over the trail completely and forming big snowdrifts where the sled frequently gets stuck.

Back home around Willow there hadn't been much opportunity to train in strong wind so I'm happy with how well the dogs are doing. But there is one strange problem that begins a little past noon. With every gust, a blast of fine snow blows up and hits Jocko and Tommy in their faces. Every time this happens, Tommy starts sneezing. Poor guy, he sneezes and sneezes so hard that we have to stop and wait for him. With each sneeze attack the dogs get a tiny break, so after Tommy's nose calms down, the dogs speed up until it happens again. After a while I move Tommy back in the team and move Amy up. Such a small thing, but it makes all the difference for Tommy and his sneezing stops.

There is only a 1/8 crescent moon and by nine in the evening clouds roll in, obscuring the faint lunar light. Within minutes our world is totally black. The good news is that the wind has finally died down and the trail is much improved. Another hour passes and I am surprised that I can see the beams of five headlamps up ahead that belong to the mushers who left two hours ahead of us. They are traveling convoy style and after a few more minutes we link up with them. I'm feeling pretty happy now because we're no longer alone on the Yukon and we're no longer trailing behind the pack.

The Yukon River is often a mile wide but this section appears much narrower in places because we are sledding past large islands. Sometime around midnight the convoy veers off the trail to the left. At first I think we must be arriving at Eagle Island but we keep going and going. Then the convoy starts swinging right then left, back and forth across the river. I call out to the musher ahead of me, "Why are we weaving back and forth?"

"We're lost. He's weaving back and forth trying to find the trail." The answer leaves me stunned. In this area locals put the trail in where they know the ice is safe and we are supposed to stay on it. To veer off the trail can be deadly because in some places the ice is as thin as a piece of tin. Sled across thin ice and you and your whole team can drop straight into the river and disappear in an instant.

About half an hour later as we weave to the right I see it! The trail! I call out, "We just sledded over the trail!"

When the musher ahead of me turns his head and looks back, I point behind me and shout, "The trail. It's back there!"

He yells in a nasty, sarcastic voice, "You want to lead this!? Huh? You want to lead!?"

What? I shout again, "The trail! It's right back there! We just crossed it!" He responds with his right hand in the air in what is clearly meant to be a rude gesture.

His behavior makes me angry but mostly I feel very nervous about what we are doing. Isn't anyone paying attention? Is everyone just following the leader? Is the leader dozing off? How could it be that none of those five mushers saw the trail? It was so obvious. I anguish over what to do. Do I stop and turn my team around? It takes a lot of room to swing back around, even with a small, nine-dog team. What if we step onto thin ice? I remember Rick Hunter's words, "There are reports of open water on the Yukon." I probably should go back but instead I decide to follow the convoy. It's a crapshoot either way.

At around 3:00 in the morning we finally arrive at the bottom of a steep riverbank at what looks like an impossibly steep trail that leads up to the cabin that is Eagle River checkpoint. Mr. Loud Mouth walks over to me, nods his head in the direction of the cabin, and says, "I don't think there's room for you and your team up there."

I don't know what the deal is with this guy. I look at him and scoff, "Why would I want to waste my dog's energy climbing up there? I'm parking my team right over there on that flat spot. If anyone has to trudge up and down that hill, it'll be me." There's no response other than a grunt as he walks away.

After checking in and cooking our food, I decide to stay with my dogs and sleep in the sled basket.

CHAPTER 20
Eagle Island to Kaltag

MARCH 18,19   **70 MILES**   **9 DOGS**

Around mid-morning the convoy-mushers take off but I decide we will wait. Nothing like the unpleasant happenings of the previous night has happened on the trail before, but to be fair, it was only the one guy who was a jerk. Nevertheless, for a while at least, I want distance between them and us.

By about two o'clock in the afternoon I figure the convoy must be far enough ahead so we can keep our distance. It's a nice trail but the usual dreaded Yukon River headwind is really strong today. Big, tall Moose keeps lowering his head and trying to turn sideways as though he is bothered by the wind, so I move him back to wheel where he will be somewhat sheltered by the other dogs' bodies. We take several breaks and the dogs wolf down lots of snacks, which keeps their energy and spirits up. Unbelievably, within four hours we catch up to the convoy spread out along the river. I wave and nod politely as my 9-dog team sleds past an eleven-dog team resting beside the trail.

River travel is always dangerous and I'm relieved to see that the ice along this stretch is strong and the trail is in good shape. But tonight I am determined that we will be following the Iditarod Trail, not someone else's sled tracks, so I keep my headlamp on continuously after dark.

A little after 10:00 in the morning, March 19, five of us arrive close together in Kaltag. It's always exciting coming into a village. People open their homes to us cold, wet, stinky mushers, and go out of their way to make everyone feel comfortable and welcome. The race is a big deal in these small villages and teachers dismiss school so the kids can be part of the event. They make big signs welcoming mushers, draw pictures of dog teams, count the dogs, ask questions, and spend a lot of time gathered around jostling each other and giggling.

Today the kids seem particularly excited and, when I ask what's going on, a chorus of voices shout, "Rick Mackey! Rick Mackey!" "Rick Mackey? What about Rick Mackey?" "He won the Iditarod!" "When?" "Last night!"

One of the adults has wandered up to greet me and fills in some exciting details. "Rick got into Nome at 11:10 last night. Finished with seven dogs. His dad was there at the finish when he won." Rick is the son of Dick Mackey who won the race in 1978. Both Rick and Dick wore bib number 13 for their starting positions. As if that isn't amazing enough, another son, Lance Mackey will wear bib number 13 when he wins the race in 2007. Yet another interesting tidbit is that Emmitt Peters wore number 13 when he won in 1975.

We talk about some of the other mushers who have finished and what they said. The best comment came from Herbie Nayokpuk. When asked by a reporter if he was happy finishing 4th, Herbie said, "I'm always happy and I'm happy with my dogs, too." No wonder he is such a crowd pleaser.

Once things settle down, I launch into the usual routine - haul water, start the Coleman stove to heat water, soak dog food in warm water, chop up a block of frozen chicken, and feed the dogs a late breakfast. Everyone is expected to be polite guests everywhere we go, so just like back home, I scoop afterwards. Admittedly, when I'm bone tired, all this work can sometimes feel like drudgery, but then when I stand back and watch those hungry sled dogs devouring their food, it takes the edge right off. There's something satisfying about watching someone eat and I think we are hard-wired to want to feed others, regardless of their species.

In the house where I stay, eating and drying things takes place downstairs and sleeping bodies are only allowed upstairs. I sit down beside Fritz Kirsch who is nursing a nasty, head cold and eating a can of frozen strawberries she purchased at the local store. I can't face another serving of Logan bread, so I speed over to the store and buy myself a can. I only met Fritz briefly one time when I was training up by Trapper Creek, a community about 45 miles north of Willow. Considering how many people are in the house, it's fairly quiet so Fritz and I sit there talking about our dogs and how traveling the Iditarod Trail hasn't been as hard as we thought it was going to be. But we also realize that being in the back of the pack allows us to take it far more easy than the mushers who are contenders and travel the entire race on almost no sleep. So far fourteen mushers have scratched for various reasons. Fritz and I hope nothing happens to make us decide to quit, but we're feeling confident about making it to Nome.

The next morning Moose eats most of his breakfast but with little enthusiasm. Tommy of course sidles over and helps the big guy clean his bowl. While waiting for the dogs to have time to digest their meal, I kneel down beside Moose and look him in the eye, "What's the matter, fella? Feeling down in the dumps?" His tail makes a tiny swish, but his eyes look a little dull. After a good going over I am stumped. He isn't dehydrated, I can't find any knots in his muscles, and the vet couldn't find anything of concern. But something isn't right. Since we are now off the river and away from the incessant wind, I hope he starts feeling better soon. But if he doesn't pick up by the next checkpoint, I will have to send him home.

CHAPTER 21
Kaltag to Unalakleet

MARCH 20, 21   **90 MILES**   **9 DOGS**

The next morning Fritz is already gone when we take off about two hours after sunrise. The Colonel and Ron Gould leave right behind us. The route takes us along the airport runway and then off into a forest of spruce trees, climbing slowly toward the 800 foot summit of the portage over to Unalakleet.

This is moose country and we are all on the lookout for them. These giants of the forest prefer willow leaves, grasses, weeds, and young tender shoots but this time of year their diet consists mainly of frozen twigs at the ends of birch and willow branches that they bite off and grind up using their large, flat teeth. The twigs are not as nutritious as grasses and leaves. By March they are struggling to keep their weight and often leave the forest to walk along trails where the going is easier. Running into a hungry, weary moose on the trail can be an annoyance that slows you down or a deadly disaster. If they decide to move off the trail, you're fine. If they refuse and you end up in a standoff, a moose might attack your team. A single strike of a moose's hoof can break a dog's leg, cave in ribs, even crush a head. As most mushers know an angry moose may not stop with your dogs; it may stomp right through the team and attack the musher. They can be deadly.

The teams slowly spread out along the trail and for a while we are by ourselves again. Within the hour my glasses are fogged up so I tuck them inside my parka pocket and my world becomes very fuzzy. The trail is well groomed and I feel relaxed, but rounding a curve I am jerked out of my reverie when I suddenly see what appears to be a large, dark object looming up ahead. I can see it's in the middle of the trail but without my glasses I can't tell what it is or if it's even moving. The dogs see it too and speed up. The gap is closing fast between us and whatever that thing is up ahead.

I remember the moose encounter back in Willow and struggle to get my glasses out but they catch on the pocket flap. *Get your glasses on!* I finally manage to yank them loose and hold them up in front of my eyes so I can at least look through the lenses. I see a head turn. I make out a face. It's Fritz! We have caught up with Fritz. Whew! She waves, I wave, and I laugh to myself. The dogs slow down and our teams travel together for a while without ever seeing a moose.

What an amazing passage this Kaltag Portage trail is. For hundreds, perhaps thousands of years, Native people from the coast and the interior have journeyed ninety miles over the Kaltag Portage to trade with one another. It's a long trek so part way along someone built a cabin known as Old Woman Cabin, where traders and now Iditarod mushers stop to rest. Fritz and I stop, snack the dogs, and go inside to warm up beside the wood stove. Actually, today the temperature is around a toasty 15-20°F outside so warming up isn't really necessary but pretty much no one passes up the chance to stop here.

A couple of people who came up here from Unalakleet on snowmachines are inside and offer us some coffee. We accept but stay only a few minutes and then carry on down the trail. A few miles later we drop down out of the hills and onto the coastal plain. What had once been an easy trail to follow now becomes a maze of snowmachine trails running every which way. To make matters worse, it is full on dark and it doesn't take long for Fritz and me to get separated. When the lights of Unalakleet finally emerge out of the darkness, my fogged up glasses are once again in my pocket and all I can see are a bunch of fuzzy blobs. Fortunately I manage to locate some trail markers. The dogs pick up the trail scent and we cruise right up to the checkpoint.

With a population of close to 800 people, Unalakleet is the biggest community between Anchorage and Nome. It's three o'clock in the morning and I'm exhausted, so race checker Victor Kotongan quickly guides me to the house where I am supposed to stay. He knocks. A few minutes later a sleepy woman opens the door and looks at him quizzically. "I've brought you your last musher," he explains. "No," the woman replies, "we've already taken in all we signed up for." "Well, it says here that you are signed up for Pam Flowers."

I look up at the woman and plead my case, "It's late. Can I just camp here for the night in front of your house? My dogs won't bark and we'll leave first thing in the morning. I promise we won't be any bother."

"No," she says with a kind smile. "You're not sleeping outside. You're coming inside. I'll draw you a bath and fix you something to eat."

"Oh, I don't need a bath or anything to eat. I just need to feed my dogs and get some sleep."

"No, a bath and some food. That's what you need."

What can you say to someone who invites an unexpected, dirty, stinky musher into their home at three o'clock in the morning and is determined to show them a bathtub and feed them a home-cooked meal? The only possible reply is to smile and say, "Thank you very much."

When I'm exhausted I find it helps me stay awake and focused if I talk out loud to myself, so I stagger around half asleep muttering as I feed the dogs and then head for the bathtub. By the time I finish bathing, a huge meal of bacon, eggs, toast, and coffee is ready. I have no appetite but this woman is so kind and gracious, no way am I going to go to bed without eating. Then she shows me to a bedroom that is all mine. No snorers! I collapse into the bed and immediately fade away into a deep, deep sleep.

In the morning I check Moose and see he hasn't gotten any perkier so I make arrangements for him to be flown back to Anchorage. While I'm hooking up my team, the musher, whose team was stuck in the brush right before the glacier, comes over to where I am staying. He tells me he has decided to scratch but before leaving wanted to thank me for helping him with his team. It's a nice gesture and I thank him for taking the time to come over for a visit.

I knock on the door and thank my host for her kindness and generosity. A few minutes later, Fritz and I meet up and head out together about half past noon.

CHAPTER 22
Unalakleet to Shaktoolik

MARCH 21　　**42 MILES**　　**8 DOGS**

By now most of the mushers have reached Nome but I'm not bothered by being in the back of the pack because we are on the coast! This is huge because I've been told that if you can make it to the coast you have a pretty good chance of making it all the way to Nome.

There is something else happening back in Anchorage that I know nothing about. I had taken quite a few days off without pay and had set out on the race flat broke. My colleagues at work knew taking part in the race was a financial struggle for me and, as I got farther along the race trail, they decided to do something to help. Someone suggested a bake sale. When a representative of the employee association went to administration and asked for permission to have the bake sale in the hospital lobby, the answer was a firm, "NO!" They did it anyway. Deborah Pugh outdid herself by baking a cake and decorating it with white frosting, miniature spruce trees, tiny cabins, two tiny mushers and ten tiny dogs. The musher in lead wore a sign that read Pam and the musher behind me had a sign that read Susan. Susan Butcher was the first woman to finish in the top twenty and this year was seeking her first win. In her Iditarod career Susan would enter 17 races and, in years to come, would win the Iditarod four times. For Deborah to put me ahead of Susan on her cake was showing a lot of faith, but since everyone knew I had no chance of being ahead of this incredible, amazing musher, it gave everyone a good laugh.

Of course, I wasn't the first person from Providence to run the Iditarod race. The indefatigable Dr. Jim Lanier worked there and the employees at the hospital were justifiably proud of him. He completed his first race in 1979 and would go on to compete in 15 more Iditarod races during a mushing career that spanned an astonishing five decades.

But I was the first "regular employee" to enter. To my colleagues, I was "one of them." They were a determined lot and their bake sale efforts were successful beyond anything they had hoped for. Later my co-worker in the Respiratory Therapy Department, Jean Kennedy, told me that during the sale so many people were bringing food in and buying food that it was almost impossible to move around in the lobby. They raised over $1,200 in one day!

Of course out on the trail I had no idea what they had been up to or that they were cheering so hard for my dogs and me. Later, when I got home after the race, what they did made all the difference in me getting back on my feet and I will be forever grateful for their kindness and generosity.

Meanwhile, back in Unalakleet, to help mushers find their way out of town a snowmachiner guides teams right up to the trail. Steve Haver and Colonel Vaughan leave about a half hour before me. When my turn comes, I shout and wave, "Thank you!" My guide calls. "Good luck!" waves and makes a U-turn back toward town. I reach the trail just before Fritz who catches up to me with her 11 dogs and after a bit passes us. For a while we travel together but since her team is faster than mine, we slowly separate.

The trail heads north on a very slick, icy road but we manage to make good time. After a few miles we swing inland among alders and start over the Blueberry Hills. Of course this section of the trail was predicted by veterans to be a really, really rough ride. They had told me there would be a series of three hills with a steep, almost straight down descent off the last hill. "Lots of big crashes on that slope." "It's the slide from hell." "Don't let your sled run over the wheel dogs." "You may want to wrap chains around your runners."

"Chains? I don't have any chains."

Silence.

"Do you have chains?"

"Well, ahh…..no," comes a reluctant reply.

"Okay then, see you later," I say cheerfully.

These mountains run along the coast for about twenty miles, so I know it isn't going to be up and over just three hills. Sure enough, as we climbed, the trail goes up and down, along a 300 foot high ridge, back down toward the beach, then through a wooded valley, up to another ridge higher than the first. On and on it goes. No matter how high we climb there seems to be some point ahead that looks even higher.

It's fairly easy to follow the stakes marking the trail but it's hard to judge distance. There are so many ups and downs, I have no idea if we are on hill one, two, or three. I keep waiting for the earth to drop out from under us so we can hurtle down the predicted "slide from hell." The dogs start sensing my stress and they seem to hesitate a little more each time we come to another uphill grade. I decide to stop for a break and give them a snack and a chance to chill out. When it's time to go, I lift the snowhook and within a couple of minutes we come to a steep downhill slope, but it's not the big one, it's just a ravine. The dogs slog across and up to the top of yet another hill and stop on their own.

From what I can see we might be on the top of the last hill but I'm not sure. The infamous drop off might be just ahead or maybe it's another hour up the trail, but I'm anxious to get going so we can get this over with. "All right," I call. Nothing. "All right." Nothing. "All right!" As if on some secret signal, the dogs all lie down.

I walk up to Jocko and ask, "What are you doing?" He casts a dismissive glance at me and then looks away as if he is saying, "What do you think I'm doing?" Tommy won't even look at me. I walk along the team, pick each dog up by their harness and plant them firmly on their feet. I walk back to my sled. "All right, lets go!" Everyone lies down. I pick them up, go back to the sled, they all lie down over and over again. I walk swiftly up to Jocko and try the lift and plant routine one more time, only this time when I pick them up, the dogs won't even unfold their legs.

This can't be happening!

By now I am in a rage, screaming at the top of my lungs, yelling unmentionable words about sled dogs and their ancestry. The dogs are not impressed by my antics. Anger is a powerful emotion, too powerful to be used around dogs so I walk away, clamp my hands on top of my head, and stare off across the hills in helpless frustration.

Minutes pass. Sigh. *Who do I think I'm kidding? I'm not in charge here. Dogs have free will and the idea that I'm in charge is nothing more than a self-imposed illusion. We're a team and I should be acting like the team captain, not some bully dictator.*

I walk briskly back to the dogs and, in a ridiculous attempt to stir up a little team spirit, start listing statistics. "Jocko, do you know one in five Iditarod teams scratch? Some mushers scratch because their dogs get sick, or the musher gets sick, or the dogs give up, or the musher gives up. Is that what you want? To be known as the lead dog who gave up and I had to scratch? Is that what you want? Well, that's not going to happen. Fourteen teams have already scratched, Jocko, and we're not going to make it 15. .....We are *not* scratching ..... if we have to stay here all night ..... we are *not scratching!*"

We may not be scratching but it's also clear we're not going anywhere either. It's time to admit that we are at a stalemate. So I slump down on my sled, fold my arms in resignation and wait. *This is so humiliating. I have no authority, I'm useless, I might as well be on another planet.*

It makes no sense to disagree with someone when they are right, even if the one that's right is a dog. Jocko has more experience in dog mushing than I do and I know he's right to declare a break. After a few more minutes I walk up and apologize. "Jocko, I'm sorry. You're right, we need to rest. We'll go when you think everyone is ready."

He looks straight ahead, then casually turns his head away and looks off over the distant horizon. It's clear he is thinking, *she has no authority, she's useless, she might just as well be on another planet.*

This is so humiliating.

Finally, after twenty, excruciatingly long minutes I walk up to Jocko and say in a matter of fact tone, "Do you think maybe we can go now, Jocko?" He turns his head away and once again looks out over the hills as though he is considering my request. Every dog is watching Jocko. Without looking at me, he sighs as if to say, "Yeah, okay," and just like that he stands up and switches from striker-dog to sled dog.

Once again, as if on some secret signal, every dog rises. They casually stretch and shake themselves off. Now that they have made their point, we are finally off again.

For the next few minutes I stand on the runners feeling a deep sense of relief and renewed hope. "We are going to do this!" I whisper under my breath.

Turns out we are near the top and in a short distance the trail drops off sharply in a steep descent. "This is it! Hang on!" We shoot past trees and rocket around curve after curve. I slam on the brake. The sled sashays side to side and starts to flip. I let off the brake. Without braking the sled edges closer and closer to Cletus and Ernie. The brush bow bumps Cletus on his behind. I stomp on the brake. Finally we reach the bottom. Only it's not quite the bottom. There is another rise. *Don't stop, don't stop! Please, please, please keep going.*

The dogs charge up, up, up and then, one last steep descent and we are on the beach! "Wahoo!"

It's still ten or twelve miles into Shaktoolik so we stop for a short breather and an emotional group hug. I move along the team telling everyone in a high, happy voice, "Good dog! You guys did great!" Everyone, even Jocko and Tommy, make eye contact and wag their tails. If dogs know anything, it's how to forgive and let bygones be bygones. All the frustration and anger that happened back up in the hills is now forgiven and we are back to being a pack of nine.

The trail into Shaktoolik is easy to follow but the wind is increasing by the minute and snow is starting to drift. It isn't cold, maybe around 5°F but as always the wind makes it feel much colder. We pull in a little after nine in the evening.

As predicted, Shaktoolik is surrounded by snowdrifts as high as houses and a powerful wind is screaming through the village. Four teams are parallel parked along a giant drift just to my left. Colonel Vaughan is standing beside a building and says, "I don't know where you are going to park your team. Every spot is taken."

"What about that spot right there?" I point to a small spot between two teams.

"It's too small, you'll never get your team in there."

"I think we can do it."

I command Jocko over toward the open spot. He comes alongside the team leader at the rear of my intended parking space at an angle. I step on the brake and call, "Jocko, all right." Without hesitation Jocko and Tommy climb up and over the snowdrift and straight into the full force of the wind blasting 25 miles per hour. "Whoa. Little bit gee." They move slightly to the right. "Whoa."

"All right," My sled moves forward until it is right in front of the leader in the team at the rear of our parking space. But it's at an angle. "Gee Jocko, gee." Jocko and Tommy swing back to the right, and then the team scrambles down to the bottom of the drift. The dogs are a little bunched up, so I keep my foot firmly on the brake and call, "All right." The team and my sled straighten out. We are now perfectly parked in a spot just big enough for my team.

I look over at Colonel Vaughan who is standing there looking at my dogs in astonishment and then he says, "Pam, your dogs will do just about anything you ask." "Well, most of the time," I reply. It's another proud moment for my dogs and me.

I get some water to soak dog food. Using the Coleman stove in wind screaming through the village at 25 miles per hour is a challenge but my sled acts as a windbreak so the stove doesn't blow out. With the food soaking, I chop big chunks of frozen beef and turkey and toss them into the bucket. I take off harnesses, booties, and check the dogs over and rub their legs and shoulders. When the food is ready, they gobble down their meal in no time and I grab up their bowls before they can blow away. In the time it takes me to stuff the bowls into my sled bag, everyone tamps down the snow with their little dog feet, then they lie down, stuff their noses under their tails, and go to sleep.

In Shaktoolik the Takaks' home is where everyone is hanging out so I hunker down into the wind and head that way. A few feet away I turn and look back at my dogs. After such a tough day, a full stomach and shelter from the wind is all they need. It never ceases to amaze me how perfectly suited sled dogs are for what they do.

At the Tataks' there are seven other mushers hanging around the kitchen table that is laden with food. It doesn't seem right to eat their food when groceries cost so much at the village store, so we take up a collection and someone goes to the store for groceries. It's crowded in the kitchen and I'm sitting in the living room talking with Colonel Vaughan when suddenly there is an uproar in the kitchen. Leroy Shank comes bursting into the living room, "Pam! Pam! You got nominated for the humanitarian award!"

"I did?" I am shocked. "Yes. None of us has ever heard of anyone in the back of the pack getting nominated for that award. That's a real honor, Pam!" "Huh. I wonder how that happened?"

The award is officially called The Leonhard Seppala Humanitarian Award. It is named in honor of Leonhard Seppala, a dog musher in Alaska during the first half of the 1900's who was known for giving outstanding care to his sled dogs and for participating in the 1925 serum run during the diphtheria epidemic in Nome. It is the most coveted of all Iditarod awards and being nominated is another proud moment for my dogs and me. This year the award will be given to Rick Mackey.

When it's time to get some sleep, I look out the window at the storm. Blowing snow strikes the window panes making a rapid tapping sound like sand tossed on tin. All night, every time I wake up, the wind is still hammering against the side of the house. I wonder if we will be able to travel tomorrow?

CHAPTER 23
Shaktoolik to Koyuk to Elim

MARCH 22,23   **96** MILES   **8** DOGS

As often happens during wind storms, morning brings a little calmer weather. When I go into the kitchen to get some coffee, everyone is talking about the next part of the trail and I'm surprised at how subdued the group is. The trail crosses Norton Bay, a huge bay on the northeast side of Norton Sound, famous for hurricane force winds and shifting ice. We are told a strong wind is moving the ice and it's starting to break up. This means teams could be carried out to sea, possibly to their deaths and, if that starts happening, we are supposed to turn and head for the nearest land as fast as possible. Exactly how we are supposed to know this is happening, I have no idea.

Before first light everyone gets busy feeding, harnessing, and booting their dogs. A snowmachiner guides Fritz out to the edge of the trail with me close behind. The rest of the overnight guests head out in quick succession. We make good time over the first nine miles of trail across windswept rolling tundra to a spit of land called Island Point.

Mindful of yesterday's debacle, I decide to rest the team and give the dogs a little snack while I check every line, harness, and booty. Before we set out across the ice, a nice friendly pep talk seems like a good idea. "Jocko, you're doing great today. Tommy, you old hound dog, how you doing? Cletus, you're looking strong today. Amy, you've become an amazing sled dog." On and on along the entire team. With every tail wagging, every dog pulling on their line, I step on the runners, lift the snowhook, and call, "All right, let's go!" With heads held high, we step out onto the ice. Koyuk is straight ahead and all we have to do to get there is cross 35 miles of breaking, shifting sea ice.

Veterans have told me that this always seems like the longest part of the trail, that it seems to take forever to get to Koyuk. I'm glad to see that the trail is well marked by a line of stakes driven into the ice. We sled over a few shallow drifts and sashay a bit over glare ice as the wind rises. I keep my eye on the coast off to the east, trying to see if we are moving away from land. It's impossible to tell. More drifts, more glare ice. We cross a narrow crack in the ice, then another and another and another. There's plenty of incentive to keep moving because so many cracks are a sign that the ice is starting to break apart. I know that wave action under the ice can break apart massive sheets of ice even faster than wind. We stop briefly so I can get off the runners. Standing on the ice, I close my eyes and try to feel if we are moving up and down. Nothing. I listen carefully for the creaking and grinding of shattering ice. Nothing.

About half way across we stop for another short break. Again I listen for signs of shifting ice but the wind is blowing so hard it's impossible to hear. There is nothing for it but to keep going. It is a long, stressful slog but at around 6:00 o'clock that evening, the dogs pull my sled off the ice and up a little rise. We have made it to Koyuk, having never floated out to sea.

As if by magic, the second we arrive kids are everywhere, asking questions, running around, chattering, playing tag, asking more questions, clearly excited by all that the race brings to their village. Like kids everywhere they are most interested in the dogs, so while the dog food is soaking I answer their questions. "What's that dogs name?" "Jocko." "Who's that?" "Tommy." "What about that one?" "Ernie." For some reason a dog being named Ernie always makes kids laugh, which makes me laugh. It feels so good to laugh. I could hang around these kids for hours, but soon darkness folds over us, and we all head for our beds.

The next morning brings a calm, beautiful day. Elim is 48 miles away along the coast, some of the trail on sea ice, some up on land. Maybe because I am starting to feel excited about getting to Nome, the dogs seem amazingly perky and happy as we head out. Ice from hell is jammed up along the shore but fortunately the trail is far enough off shore to skirt around most of it. In the distance I can see a sheer-walled 500 foot high chunk of rock that some people still call Castle Rock, but in 1921 the name was officially changed to Bald Head. The trail turns inland before the headland and we easily sled up and over a few hills which, thank heavens, the dogs cross without going on strike. Maybe it's the mild temperature, running around 5°F, maybe it's that the hills aren't very high, but the dogs are clipping right along and seem to be enjoying themselves.

Five miles of smooth ice brings us to Moses Point, a sandy four-mile long spit of land. From there the trail turns inland for several miles, climbing up and over some bluffs. It's a happy, easy run and we arrive in Elim at about 5:30 p.m.

Once the dogs are checked over, fed, and bedded down for the night, I'm invited to spend the evening with a family who serves a delicious meal of reindeer with all the trimmings. They offer to take me by snowmachine up to a hot springs but I'm just too tired. Normally I'm a very quiet person around other people and now I'm afraid I'm not a very good guest. I explain that I am really tired and need to get some sleep. My hosts smile kindly and say they understand.

CHAPTER 24
Elim to Golovin to White Mountain

MARCH 24, 25   **46 MILES**   **8 DOGS**

For some reason everyone is slow getting up the next morning and my dogs and I are no exception. There's no shortage of kids though and they help perk us up. Finally, I wave goodbye and move swiftly out onto the sea ice. Another beautiful day makes for a pleasant run of about 8 miles along the coast past Walla Walla, a one-time roadhouse along the Iditarod Trail. Two or three miles farther and we turn inland at a cabin. The route ahead goes into the Kwiktalik Mountains up to an elevation of about 1,000 feet on what mushers call Little McKinley. Once again warning bells clang loudly in my brain. "This is the worst yet." "Don't count on making it to Nome until after you've gotten over Little McKinley." "It's a rough climb up but wait until the downhill." "It's a nightmare. You'll see."

Okay, okay, I'm sufficiently traumatized by yet another dire warning. My mind flips back to the dog strike from a couple of days ago so we stop by the cabin for a snack and some rest while I ponder what lies ahead. After careful consideration I make a little speech announcing my decision. "Jocko, Tommy, don't take this wrong but I'm making some changes. You two have led almost the entire way so I'm giving you both a rest. Cletus and Amy are going to run up front for a while."

No one seems to mind being moved around, so I step on the sled and call, "All right, let's go!"

What a fiasco. Amy is the most brilliant dog I have ever known. She's a spark plug of a dog and her enthusiasm keeps us going when things start getting dull. But reliable she is not and today she refuses to keep her tug line taut. Cletus is a big, happy-go-lucky dog who is strong enough to pull me to Nome all by himself. It's the happy-go-lucky part of his personality that's the problem today. He and Amy start playing as we move at a glacial speed along the trail. The playfulness begins to spread through the team and soon we are having dog recess.

"You two did pretty well in lead the other day, so what's the deal?" Cletus wags his tail and starts playing with Amy like he has forgotten he's a sled dog. "Okay, let's try something different, shall we?" I give Sasha a chance to work beside Amy but she is too shy to take up the responsibility of being a leader and folds back between Tommy and Jocko. Maybe it was all those kids playing around and being happy back in Elim, but I just cannot bring myself to get upset.

Obviously, Amy just isn't in the mood to be a lead dog today so I decide that it's probably not a good idea to rearrange the troops when we are facing yet another Iditarod trauma. So back to the usual lineup - Jocko and Tommy, Sasha and Amy, Hank and Ed, Ernie and Cletus. Off we go. It's about a mile-long climb up 1,000 feet to the top of the ridge. I stay off the runners and push the sled to help the dogs. Admittedly it's a struggle but we get to the top and take a breather, more for me than the dogs.

On Little McKinley for every mile up there must be three miles down. The trail is a snowmachine trail full of humps and bumps and the snow is snot-slick. I don't know how long our descent will take but I keep the brake on during the entire rocket ride back down to sea level. "Wahoo!" We make it to the bottom in one piece and stop for a little rest. I hop off the sled and walk along the team, starting with Cletus and Ernie. "You guys really pulled hard. Hank, Ed you two kept your nose to the snow and didn't stop even once to sniff around. Sasha, Amy, great work!" Finally, "Jocko, Tommy, without you two we'd still be back in Willow. Dogs, we are going to make it to Nome!" Okay, so I enjoy my dogs and get kind of mushy sometimes but we're doing it. One more hurdle is now behind us.

In Golovin I cannot find the checker or checkpoint, so I ask someone walking along the street where we should go. She points to a house so I drive the team over and park. I'm the only one there so checker Bobby Amarok quickly goes over everything and signs me in. Mary Amarok is very kind and offers me spaghetti and fruit cocktail, which I happily devour. It's only 5:00 o'clock and I am anxious to cover the 18 miles to White Mountain, so we stay only about an hour.

Out of Golovin we move along a beautiful, straight, hard-packed trail, wind around a bit on the Fish River delta and pull into White Mountain about 8:30 p.m. I can hardly believe we made it so fast. By midnight ten teams are resting in White Mountain, all taking their mandatory four hour rest break. Everyone is over the top excited. Nome is just 77 miles away!

CHAPTER 25

White Mountain to Safety

MARCH 25   52 MILES   8 DOGS

O f course the veteran's forecast network calls for trauma along the White Mountain to Safety leg. "Blue sky one minute, screaming blizzard the next." "It's a blow hole." "Winds strong enough to blow you right off your sled. You'll see."

"But the forecast is for good weather, not much wind."

"That's just the forecast. Weather out there can change in a heartbeat."

"Okay, I'll be careful."

"Then there's Topkok to get over. Oh that's a tough one. You'll see."

I raise my eyebrows, sigh, and say with a wry smile, "It's always something."

My dogs and I leave about six a.m., just as dawn arrives. There is no wind and the trail is well marked with stakes along the Fish River. We head over land and up the Topkok River. Still no wind. The gods are smiling on us from a sunny sky, 20°F., and blowing just enough breeze to keep us cool.

The dogs sense my joy and move at a steady pace, pulling me up and over a series of ridges to the top of Topkok. The horrific winds that were predicted are blowing somewhere else today so we stop for a rest. Also missing is snow. The teams and snowmachines that have run over this section of trail before us have ground it down to dirt. The "trail" is nothing more than a slight rut but at least there's still something to follow.

Oh, but the view! It is spectacular! Framed by the massive sea ice of Norton Sound on the left, Cape Nome straight ahead, and rolling snow-covered hills to the right, all under a brilliant, cloudless blue sky. It is one of those moments that is so perfect, so mesmerizing, you want to stop time and simply be, so for a few minutes we do just that.

But we cannot stay here. Fifteen miles past the headland of Cape Nome is the finish line waiting for us, pulling us forward. Almost in a whisper I call, "All right, let's go," and we sled down to the coast.

Moving steadily along the trail, thinking back over the past few days, I feel a mix of emotions. Of course I'm happy that we are going to make it to Nome but I gotta say I'm feeling a little bit cheated. I was figuring on having a few more stories about death-defying feats on the trail to tell people back home. We were supposed to fight and struggle and suffer over the last hundred miles. I mean all those veterans told me that's how it would be. They promised. Now I'm wondering will anyone believe me when I tell them that we climbed Little McKinley, sledded through the blow hole, and zipped up and over Topkok with the greatest of ease?

But there are no missing stories; the story is my dogs and me traveling together across a thousand miles of Alaska through bad times and good.

Dusk has fallen as we pull into Safety. The checker is a man from England bursting with enthusiasm who gives me a huge, bear hug and hearty congratulations. Nothing could have surprised me more than when he said, "We just caught some fish and we're gonna have a fish fry. Stay and have fish with us."

My mind is locked on a burled arch just 22 miles away. "Oh, thank you, but I really want to get back on the trail and get to Nome."

"Oh, but the fish is fresh! You have to stay!"

"No, really. Thanks but I need to go."

"Look at them, don't they smell wonderful?" He holds out the frying pan, waves his hand, and the scent rises up my nose and straight into my stomach. "They're already cooked. Please, just sit down and eat."

He is so insistent and such a happy, delightful man, and after days of mostly Logan bread, spaghetti, and fruit cocktail, I have to admit a dinner of freshly cooked fish sounds pretty good. I can't believe I'm doing this, but I sit down as he slides two fish onto a plate and sets them in front of me. There is another musher across the table who succumbs to temptation instead of tending to business, but he will remain unnamed and I'll leave it up to him if he wishes to come forward and confess later.

Within minutes we are busted. The Safety radio operator informs Nome that we have arrived but that we are staying for a fish fry.

I have to admit my fellow musher and I are a little embarrassed when we hear a voice shouting over the radio, "WHAT! What do you mean they're having a fish fry??? You tell those two to get on their sleds and get back on that trail right now!"

It had been a perfect run through perfect weather and now we are eating perfectly cooked fish. In sled dog style, I quickly wolf down the fish. Then, with great ceremony, I rise, look at our checkpoint chef, and say, "Duty calls and I must answer." We all burst out laughing as I head for the door.

A musher approaches the famous
burled arch which is the finish line
for the Iditarod race.

At the finish of the race a local radio
announcer interviews me.

The coveted Iditarod belt buckle is
awarded to mushers upon completing
their first Iditarod. They receive only one
belt buckle no matter how many times
they complete the race.

Every musher who finishes the race
receives an Iditarod finisher's patch.
A patch is given every time a musher
finishes a race.

CHAPTER 26
Safety to Nome

MARCH 26   **25 MILES**   **8 DOGS**

I t's very dark when we leave for Nome but the trail is well marked and easy to follow. We seem to be completely alone when all of a sudden we sled up a small rise and suddenly there are people on snowmachines riding along beside us and I can hear an air raid siren in the distance. The noise and lights are a little startling but, hey, it's been a perfect day, so I go with the flow.

After a bit I manage to make out some people alongside the street. When I finally get my glasses on, I see it's a crowd, a really big crowd. People are cheering. "What on earth?" Then I remember it's Friday night. A peek at my watch tells me it's just becoming Saturday so of course the bars have emptied out to celebrate the arrival of another musher. It doesn't matter that I am the fifty-first musher to arrive, the people just want to celebrate that someone, anyone is finishing the Iditarod.

There are so many people that I can't figure out where to go. We are supposed to sled under the famous burled arch that marks the end of the Iditarod Sled Dog Race, but I can't find the thing. What appears to be a wall of people confuses Jocko, too, so he moves over to the right and stops in front of a smiling woman. "Haw, Jocko, haw," I call but with all the noise he can't hear me so I jump off the sled, run up and take him by the harness. "It's okay Jocko, I don't know where to go either."

As I guide Jocko back to the middle of the street, I look ahead and suddenly - there it is! Right in front of us - the arch! I hop on the sled and off we go on the last few yards. My dogs and I have sledded 1,000 miles in 20 ½ days for the privilege of sledding under that arch! Jocko and Tommy's noses cross the finish line and it's over! We did it! We have finished the Iditarod Sled Dog Race!

After the checker and I go through my sled for the final time, I sign the form and then turn to my dogs. I need to move out of the way because there will soon be other mushers finishing. There's a problem. I can't find my dogs! "My dogs! Where are my dogs?" Mayor Leo Rasmussen assures me, "They're fine. The radio announcer wants to interview you."

"But my dogs! Where are they?" We've been together non-stop for three weeks and I feel panicked that I can't find them.

The Mayor finally realizes I'm not going to do the interview until I know where my dogs are and he offers a quick explanation. "It's okay, Pam, your dogs are okay. Volunteers have taken them down the street. They'll unharness them, give them a bed of straw, and hang your harnesses on your sled. Your dogs are okay."

I finally calm down and the radio announcer, who has a huge tape recorder hanging from his shoulder, aims his microphone at me. "We're live. Can you tell me a brief story about something interesting that happened out on the trail?"

"Yes. We were on The Burn and we came to a fork in the trail and I couldn't decide which way to go. It was really cold and windy so I was hunkered down with my dogs waiting for daylight when along came Saul Paniptchuk. He stopped to check on me and told me he was going to take whichever trail his lead dog chose. I decided to follow Saul and his leader chose the right trail. I really appreciated him helping me that night, so if Saul is out there listening, I want to give him a big thank you."

In that moment the crowd parts and there stands Saul! "Saul!" He walks over with his hand stuck out about ten feet in front of him, beaming a smile that covers his entire face. We shake hands, the crowd cheers and claps and cheers some more.

It is a perfect ending to a perfect day.

When things settle down I ask to be taken to my dogs so I can check on them and someone kindly leads me down to where they are resting. Sure enough, as promised and predicted, they are unharnessed, curled up, and snoozing away on huge piles of straw. One by one, I kneel beside each dog, stroking them, massaging their legs, whispering their names, telling them what great dogs they are. They barely stir. Satisfied that they are safe and comfortable, I follow my host to her house where I sleep soundly in a warm, clean bed.

The next day after feeding my dogs, I have lunch with Saul and a few other mushers. We are all blown away by how excited people are and how they turn out to greet every one of us no matter what position we finish in. We reminisce about all the things that happened on the trail and speculate about what we plan to do next. Then we shake hands and head our separate ways.

The motto for the race is The Last Great Race on Earth. It truly is that and more. My dogs and I were a close team when we started but, out there along the trail, a deeper bond formed between us than I ever thought possible. We learned to work together, to depend on each other, and we learned to respect one another. Completing the Iditarod Trail Sled Dog Race with these amazing and beautiful dogs remains one of the greatest highlights of my life.

Along the trail hundreds of volunteers from Anchorage to Nome helped take care of us and made the race possible and successful. People shared their homes and meals with us for no reason other than they just wanted to help. In this race 68 teams started out of Anchorage and 54 managed to finish. I was 51 out of those 54 and yet people greeted my dogs and me at the finish as though I had won. They greeted everyone who finished with the same enthusiasm. I met and spent time with so many amazing mushers who truly cared about their dogs and loved being with them. They taught me so much.

I thank everyone who helped and shared and cheered and brought joy to themselves and to us.

EPILOGUE

Dreams are a great source of power. They give us inspiration and help us believe in ourselves. Best of all, dreams give us hope that the future will be better.

Of course often times life doesn't come close to the dreams we hold in our heads, but sometimes it does. Ever since I was a young girl I dreamed of dog sledding across miles of vast wilderness. Now that dream has come true and it turned out to be bigger and better than anything I ever imagined.

Over the next three decades my dogs and I would go on many extreme, arctic expeditions. Sometimes we were adrift on arctic sea ice for days, climbed pressure ridges over 25 feet high, fended off polar bears, and traveled alone for weeks often hundreds of miles from the nearest human being. Always my dogs and I worked together as a team.

The following pages give a brief look at some of those expeditions.

Two years later Amy and that rascal Tommy got together and produced a beautiful litter of puppies, ensuring a future in dog mushing for us.

My first attempt to reach the North Pole was thwarted by endless pressure ridges ranging from eight to over twenty five feet.

An uninvited visitor did not stop us from reaching the Magnetic North Pole.

Rubble ice often slowed us down on our 2,500 mile trans-arctic expedition.
There was never a trail but we always found a way through.

Icebergs sometimes provided a temporary respite from the constant winds
on our 2,500 mile trans-arctic expedition.

Ten years after my Iditarod race, eight dogs and I sledded 2,500 miles alone across Arctic America from Barrow (now known as Utqiagvik) to Repulse Bay on the east side of Canada, retracing the route of famous arctic explorer Knud Rasmussen. There was no trail on this entire crossing. We set a record for the longest solo dog sled expedition by a woman and the first American to cross the Arctic alone by dog team. My dogs and I overcame every challenge and succeeded in achieving our goal of crossing the Arctic. Led by Douggie, son of Iditarod dogs Amy and Tommy, seven of the eight dogs on this journey were descendants of the dogs in my Iditarod team.

This expedition is the subject of the book *Alone across the Arctic.*

In 2008 My dog, Ellie, and I set out to realize another of my dreams. We thru-hiked the approximately 2,200-mile Appalachian Trail, hiking north to south over the winter in 199 days.

This journey is the subject of the book *Ellie's Long Walk*.

What dreams are next?

That's for each of us to decide.

Glossary

BRUSH BOW: A piece of wood or plastic that wraps around the front of a dog sled.

COME GEE: The command that tells the lead dog to turn around to the right and go back the direction from which it came.

COME HAW: The command that tells the lead dog to turn around to the left and go back the direction from which it came.

COMMANDS: The words used by mushers to tell their lead dogs what to do.

GANGLINE: A system of ropes running from the front of the dogsled. The dogs are clipped into the gangline by lines called tug lines.

GEE: The command that tells a dog to turn right.

GLARE ICE: Smooth, glassy ice that is very slick and difficult to stand up on.

HAW: The command that tells a dog to turn left.

HYPOTHERMIA: A condition in which the body becomes too cold to maintain its normal temperature and shuts down the flow of blood to hands and feet, then arms and legs, in an attempt to keep vital organs warm.

LEAD: An opening in sea, river, or lake ice.

MOUNT McKINLEY: The tallest mountain in North America. Its formal name has been changed to Denali.

MUSH: To be pulled over snow and ice on a sled pulled by dogs.

MUSHER: A person who rides on a dog sled and commands the dog team, also called a dog driver.

PRESSURE RIDGE: A ridge of ice. commonly ranging in height from a few feet up to twenty feet or more, formed by the pressure of expanding or shifting ice.

SEA ICE: Ice that forms when ocean water freezes.

SIBERIAN HUSKY: A medium-size breed of dog with a thick, soft coat, erect ears, and a bushy tail originating from Siberia. They are known for being friendly, hard-working, and are often used to pull a dog sled.

SLED BAG: A heavy cloth bag that is placed in the sled basket and cinched tightly to contain gear and keep snow out.

SLED BASKET: The main body of the sled where passengers or cargo are carried.

SLED BRAKE: A two or three-pronged metal claw attached to the floor of the sled used to stop or slow the sled when pressed down by the musher. A spring holds the brake up when not in use.

SNOWHOOK: A large, heavy, two-pronged, iron hook attached to the sled with a rope that is used to anchor the sled by jamming the prongs into the snow.

TOW LINE: The line that runs down the middle of the gangline and is attached to the sled.

TUG LINE: A rope that is attached at one end to the dog's harness and the other end to the gangline.

TUNDRA: Treeless plains in the arctic with low-growing vegetation on top of cold, often frozen ground.

Pam Flowers lives near Talkeetna, Alaska where she enjoys hiking, back-packing, snowshoeing, and reading with her Labrador retriever, Gracie.

She is the author of eight books, has participated in nine arctic expeditions, most of them solo, reached the Magnetic North Pole three times, completed the Iditarod Sled Dog Race, dog sledded 2,500 miles alone across Arctic America, and thru-hiked the Appalachian Trail.

Most years she travels as a visiting author to elementary schools in the Lower 48 and does presentations about her expeditions. Pam has visited nearly 1,500 schools and over 200 libraries across America.

She has no plans to retire.